# GULLIBLE'S TRAVELS

# GULLIBLE'S
# TRAVELS

*MARY BODELL*

*WITH DRAWINGS BY VASILIU*

DODD, MEAD & COMPANY
NEW YORK

914.2
B63g

July, 1963

TO MY HUSBAND

# CONTENTS

# GULLIBLE'S TRAVELS

# 1. THE HARD WAY

IN THE NEW ENGLAND TOWN WHERE I GREW UP DURING THE
twenties, it was considered meritorious, for some never
divulged reason, to do everything the hard way. You didn't
use canned foods unless you had canned them yourself;
you never heated the bedrooms in the winter but you always opened a window; you prepared for the worst, having no doubt that it would arrive; you wore out your old

clothes and saved your new ones until they were old when it was all right to wear them. Wear it out; use it up; make it do! Thus you saved money. And when you had it, you didn't spend it. You held on to it.

Being lazy was bad. Working hard was good. My brother and I picked potato bugs and dropped them into a jar containing a little kerosene. A jarful was worth a nickel. Ashes from the furnace were spread on a pathway beside the house, and if we were seen being lazy, we were handed a pail by our grandmother and told to pick up the pieces of unburned coal. A pailful was worth a nickel. My grandmother was not of old New England stock; she was from Alsace-Lorraine, which is just as bad.

In school we were further indoctrinated in this way of life by memorization of poems like "Aladdin" by James Russell Lowell, which celebrates the ineffable pleasures of poverty and damp cellars, and "The Landing of the Pilgrim Fathers" by Felicia Hemans. I still fondly remember my eighth grade English teacher, a sterling rock-ribbed woman throwing everything she had, which was considerable, into a thundering rendition of "Be Strong!": "Be strong!" went the poem,

"We are not here to play, to dream, to drift!
We have hard work to do and loads to lift!"

The trouble with such an upbringing is that it sticks. It sticks to the personality just as clam chowder, baked beans and New England boiled dinners stick to the ribs. It certainly stuck to me, anyway, with the result that in these days of easy living and frozen and prepared everything, I am a sad anachronism, especially since we make our home in Southern California, the land of *everybody's* future, where even the climate makes me feel guilty!

Although in daydreams, I have sometimes wallowed in luxury and ease, in reality, when given a choice, I always take the hard way. That's probably why I am sitting here now pounding this out when I could just as well be with the sybarites in beauty parlor or specialty shop, spending their husbands' hard-earned money.

I was lucky in finding Pete, a strong handsome man who likes to do things the hard way, too, and who promptly proved it by marrying me. The day after our wedding, I had to go back to finish my senior year at Radcliffe (that's where I started and that's where I was going to finish!) and he went back to Baltimore where he was working. It was a satisfactorily hard beginning, but we spent most of our money on planes, trains and hotel rooms in New York. That year over, he joined the Navy, and we began the process of having six children in various parts of the United States. I nursed all the children, and if you saw me, you'd find another example of doing things the hard way. I am not a fecund-looking type nor did I ever overflow with either milk or honey.

So when my husband applied, in the fall of 1955, for a Guggenheim Fellowship so that he could spend his sabbatical year (1956–1957) working with Professor Holberg in Copenhagen and the following summer seeing Europe with me and the children, I was raring to go. It would be, in a way, the consummation of a life spent doing things the hard way.

The children were going through difficult stages of development for the most part. Helen, the oldest, was thirteen, extremely stubborn and given to philosophy and soul-searching. The child of hopelessly benighted, bird-brained and reactionary parents and fighting them every inch of the way, she had blossomed forth as an intellectual, a fierce free soul, a champion of the oppressed, a Show-er of the Way. One look at her in the midst of a splendid moment, her blue eyes blazing, her golden hair sending off sparks, her sturdy shoulders set, her strong chin determined, was enough to wilt me instantly.

Katy, a year younger, was the opposite of her sister. She was willowy and athletic. The backs of her socks always managed to disappear into the backs of her shoes. This never bothered her; she just walked on the lumps. Her slip showed. Her blouse was never tucked into her skirt. According to Helen, she was neither politically nor intellectually aware, and she didn't give a darn. If there was anything breakable near her, she broke it; anything full of liquid, she spilled it; anything on the floor to fall over, she fell over it. Katy thought I worried unnecessarily about everything—Helen thought I didn't worry enough about *important* things—and often gave me a cheerful pat on the back which nearly knocked me over, murmuring meanwhile, "Just take it easy, Ma!"

Jean, at seven, liked everybody, animal and human, and everybody liked her. She had musical talent and an allergy to fur and hence was extremely sensitive. We could scold the others, but if we said a sharp word to Jean, she grew exceedingly quiet, seeming to shrink, and her big gray eyes slowly filled with tears.

Mike had his problems, the first and foremost being that he was the only boy among five girls. His position in the family was worrisome to me because it was the same as Branwell Brontë's—fourth place after Maria, Elizabeth and Charlotte and before Emily and Anne—and everybody knows what happened to poor Branwell. Mike would be six during our year in Denmark and thus he would miss first grade and learning to read English. We would have to teach him how to read, evenings.

Ruthie, four, presented few problems as yet, but Alice was not only a baby, she was The Baby and destined to be spoiled. Also, it could be guaranteed that she would be wearing diapers the whole time we were away.

At the time he applied for a grant, Pete, being foresighted and optimistic, also had booked two staterooms on the S.S. *America*, leaving New York for Bremerhaven, Germany, on September 11, 1956. This worried me. I didn't doubt he'd get a Guggenheim, but "Don't count your chickens before they're hatched" was another axiom often used in New England.

As March of 1956 began, we still hadn't heard from the Guggenheim Foundation. Some at UCLA had received various grants and were busily making plans. It was nerve-racking to wait. Each evening when Pete came home, I very carefully avoided asking him, knowing that if he'd had good news, he'd have shouted it the minute he came through the door. He appreciated my not asking. Occasionally but with false heartiness, we talked about what we'd do with our sabbatical if the Guggenheim didn't come through.

Meanwhile, I was going on doggedly doing my best to make things hard for myself at home, eschewing mixes and frozen foods, not driving when I could walk, getting down on hands and knees to wash floors so as to keep myself from getting stiff and lazy, putting things away on high shelves so I'd have to stretch. In these and other ways I earned merit and stars in my heavenly crown, and I also saved money since I was getting exercise I'd otherwise have to pay for in gymnasiums and bowling alleys. The value of these Spartan tactics has been questioned by members of the household, even sometimes by me, but at least I will have reared five daughters who would not stoop to using cake mixes and a son who'll make some girl a fussy husband.

Then, one morning in early March, I was bathing the baby in the bathtub (to get the benefits of bending over) when Ruthie called upstairs to me that there was a man at the door. It was a postman with a fat special delivery letter from the John Simon Guggenheim Foundation. I turned it over and over with shaking fingers and tried to read through the envelope, gave up finally and telephoned my husband. I have never got into the bad habit of opening his mail. It's generally bills—that's why.

"Well, open it!" he said.

"I'm afraid to," I told him.

"Oh, for God's sake, open it!" he said. It proved to be

a number of confusing forms and a request for an estimate of expenses.

"That's it!" he said triumphantly. "I'll be right home for lunch."

So we got our chance to do things the hard way in Europe, even to camping for three months from Norway to Spain. (I thought up *this* idea one mad night in March and Pete latched on to it.)

I was too elated at first to worry about the difficulties the year ahead presented. And during the summer while Pete taught summer school, I was too busy. Our large messy house had to be put into condition for renting. I had to shop and pack in a planned and economical way, preparing for every eventuality. All this had to be done when school was out and I had six little helpers at home.

One day in August, about a week before our departure by plane for New York, I was doing some last minute shopping in Westwood with Skilly Stone who was also about to go off on sabbatical with her husband, Hosmer. The Stones are well-known at UCLA for doing everything the hard way, too—one summer, on a camping vacation in Washington State, they picked and canned twenty-seven quarts of blueberries. So understandably, they have always been proud of us.

We ran into a friend of Skilly's and Skilly introduced me, adding, "Mary and her husband are taking their six children to Denmark on sabbatical!"

The woman's jaw dropped. She backed away a bit.

"What's more," said Skilly, admiringly, "they're going

to spend next summer *camping* all through Europe!"

"Oh my!" whispered the woman. She obviously thought we were dangerously mad. "And my husband and I won't even take our two to the zoo in San Diego!"

Through the next twelve months, this remark gave me plenty of food for thought.

# 2. THE KIEL CANAL

I ALWAYS THOUGHT MY HUSBAND MUST HAVE HAD SOME
sort of mystical experience in junior high school. Onaway
Junior High in Shaker Heights, Ohio, sometime in 1931 or
1932. Whatever it was, that period of his life gleamed
splendidly for him and its clouds of glory have trailed along
with him ever since, occasionally bedewing our life together.

9

For instance, I have never been able to make tuna fish and noodles the way they used to make it in the cafeteria of Onaway Junior High School. When we were first married, I tried, God knows! I made it with wide noodles, thin noodles, spaghetti, and spaghettini, with cheese and/or mushrooms, without cheese and/or mushrooms. I made it runny and I made it stiff.

"It's good," he'd say of each variation.

"But is it like Onaway Junior High School?" I'd demand.

"Well, to be perfectly frank," he'd say, "no!"

Likewise, there was the burnt sugar cake he used to eat at Onaway Junior High School. Mine was ambrosia, of course, but it didn't have quite the same taste. Now, a good many brides must try to measure up to their mother-in-law's cooking, but I never had that trouble. In fact, my mother-in-law had to take a back seat to Onaway Junior High School, too. "It used to make me so mad!" she said. "I tried and tried all the time he was in high school. I don't know why I didn't ask for the recipe. I guess that would have been giving in!"

Through sixteen years of married life, I never knew my husband had a passion for the Kiel Canal until we were about to go to Denmark. The easiest way to get to Denmark from Los Angeles is to fly over the Pole, especially when you have six children ranging in age from eleven months to thirteen years. But we were going to go by plane to New York, by ship to Bremerhaven, Germany, where we would pick up a Volkswagen bus and drive up through Schleswig-Holstein, across the Kiel Canal, across the peninsula of Jutland, across the island of Funen, and thence to Copenhagen.

The children would certainly enjoy the life on shipboard, Pete said, and it would be a good rest for me, especially after having done all that packing and cleaning to get the house ready to rent. I looked forward to those carefree days aboard ship, too. But, I asked, why couldn't we just take a ship all the way to Copenhagen and buy our Volkswagen there?

"What?" he said, "and miss that trip through Germany and the Kiel Canal?"

"What's so great about the Kiel Canal anyway?" I asked. "Surely it doesn't compare with such engineering feats as the Suez and Panama Canals."

"I don't know exactly," he said, "I've always been fascinated by the Kiel Canal. I read a book about it when I was a kid."

What kind of fearful fascination could the Kiel Canal hold for a man who had once done shore patrol in the red-light district of Hong Kong?

"*When* exactly did you read that book?" I demanded.

"I think it was back in Onaway Junior High School," he said.


So there we were, the last ones trickling off the ship in Bremerhaven on a Sunday morning. We had dug ourselves into the two staterooms so well that I don't know how we ever pulled ourselves together. Then there had been fond good-bys to the attendant in the children's playroom, the nurse and the stewards, especially our steward in the tourist-class dining salon. He was a Filipino named Arrigo, and undoubtedly the most inept but eager to please of all the stewards. He had probably been assigned to us for that reason and ours was the only table he served. Whatever we ordered, he brought us something else, and then to make up for it, he brought us everything. Inevitably we had to leave a table burdened with little dishes of untouched cole slaw, sliced tomatoes, preserved figs and melted wrong kind of ice cream.

"What do you do with all the stuff that's left over?" I asked him once.

"Feed the fishies!" he giggled. "By-by garbage!"

Appalled by all the waste, I tried my best to have him bring only what we ordered. I underlined the dishes on the menu, and put big fat 2's and 3's beside them to indicate the number of servings. Then I attempted to go over the order with him. He would nod smilingly and then bring us what he wanted to. I once mentioned my methods which didn't work to another steward. "Good old Arrigo," he said, "he can write reading, but he can't read writing!"

A steward like that you don't just casually leave. Especially when you have to take kids out into a strange country, feed them, and bed them, and all in German. Standing up on the first-class deck the night before because our deck was busy with unloading, looking at the foreign lights and the men bustling around with important uniform caps on their heads, listening to the "Achtungs!" tolled out at frequent intervals from the docks with floods of incomprehensible hissings and growlings following them, I was suddenly overcome by the enormity of what we were doing.

"Do you realize we have to get out in the middle of *that* tomorrow morning?" I asked.

"We'll manage," Pete said absently, gazing northeast to the Kiel Canal.

We managed. When we finally left the ship, the dock was pretty well cleared of crowds. The man from the auto agency had arrived half an hour before with our bus. With frightening efficiency we were swept into it, driven to the agency where we signed the papers and within an hour, there we were heading northeast, vibrating over the cobblestones of the narrow Nieder Sachsen roads. Huge trucks, some with trailers, smaller three-wheeled trucks, little buglike cars and bicycles—all with *Germans* in them—roared past us, and my husband hadn't quite got the hang of the different gearshift.

Even on a sunny morning the North German landscape looks gloomy. The countryside was rankly, wetly green, the fields harvested and blank. There was a look of sullen secrecy about the dark red brick farmhouses, huge with thatched roofs, and tiny windows thickly curtained. The forests looked black and thick. I could imagine Saxons with horns lurking in them. We were dressed all wrong, I could tell, from the people we saw in the towns. My husband's pants were much too narrow in the leg. His shoes were black and they should have been bright tan. As for me, I didn't match rigidly enough with regard to shoes, gloves, purse and hat, and, in this land of the D-cup, my brassiere was about three sizes too meager.

The children did not seem to feel self-conscious at all. Helen and Katy thought that *they* were dressed right and all the German girls wrong. The little ones were delighted with the bus; it was so roomy and the seats were fine for climbing over. I kept trying to teach them the German words for animals and things we saw, but they were too excited to pay attention.

"When are we going to get to the Kiel Canal, Daddy?" Mike asked.

"Oh, not till tomorrow! And *then*, you'll see something, you can bet!"

"Oh boy," yelled Mike.

"I can hardly wait," I said sourly. I was terrified at the idea of climbing out of the bus, followed by six exotic children and a husband with too short hair and too narrow pants, and actually going into a restaurant and trying to order something. The only German food word I could remember was sauerkraut and nobody liked sauerkraut but Helen and me.

We went through the ordeal at Stade, a pleasant spick-and-span town on the Elbe, and it turned out not to be such an ordeal after all. There was a moat around the town —at least we took it for a moat—with grassy banks and trees. There were window boxes of geraniums on some of the shop fronts. The houses were the oldest we had ever seen and Pete took pictures. We ate in a small restaurant and the proprietor spoke good English, so I relaxed, and smiled at the patrons who were smiling at me. The children behaved perfectly.

"It's not going to be so bad," I said when we were back in the bus. "I'll bet we find someone who speaks English wherever we stop." Besides, some of my college German was coming back to me. Pete said his was, too. "Have you two double rooms?" he asked in German.

"*Bitte!*" I said, "You always forget to say 'Please.' "

In the fields there were black and white cows up to their knees in rich green grass. We saw an old man in his Sunday suit going visiting on a bicycle with a bunch of flowers in its basket, and two very old ladies with shawls on their heads sitting silent together in the sun. This brought tears to my eyes. My grandmother used to go visiting on Sunday afternoons, carrying a bunch of flowers. Or aged ladies from the old country came to our house, in their good black dresses, shawls over their heads, and they sat in the kitchen drinking coffee and eating *kuchen*, talking and weeping over their youth in Alsace-Lorraine. I'd be given the stiff bunch of bachelor's buttons, marigolds and zinnias, tied tightly with string, to stick in a vase. They'd pat me on the head and call me *liebchen*. I hadn't seen an old lady for years, because nobody gets that old in our country—they're always seventy or eighty years young.

We planned to spend the night in Neumünster. We reached it around five o'clock. It had been clouding up for the last hour and Neumünster looked romantic in the gray light, just as I'd always pictured a German town. The signs were Gothic, the streets were brick, the houses and stores in the center of town presented a solid three and four story front, tapering up to steep tiled roofs. We decided to eat at the railroad station restaurant and inquire there about a good hotel.

Sad to say, it looked like any old railroad station restaurant inside. When we walked in, everybody stared. We huddled together, waiting, and finally after a hurried conference with a couple of waiters, the manager ushered us into a big room to the side, a bleak room with none of the tables set up. A waiter presented us with menus and hastily set our table. Meanwhile we stared aghast at words we'd never seen before. Everything looked suspiciously as if it would turn out to be pigs' knuckles or have sauerkraut in it. There wasn't even a *wiener schnitzel*, although never again did we fail to find *wiener schnitzel* on a German menu.

The waiter had disappeared. Smoke, laughter and the smell of cooking, a great blaze of warmth and *gemütlichkeit* came through the doors from the main room into our coldness and our lonely inadequacy. I had a can of baby food for Alice that I wanted warmed. Nobody came. Alice puckered up, tears squeezed out of her eyes. She said, "Eat!" and "Daddy!" Her only words. Nobody came.

Finally I got up the courage to venture forth. The buzz of conversation stopped. All eyes were on me and my can of liver and bacon. Everybody listened in fascination while I explained in English to the proprietor, who said he understood some English, what should be done with the can of baby food. He summoned a little blonde girl who listened big-eyed while he translated my directions. She threw one pitiful look at me and skittered back into the kitchen, holding the baby food as if it were an asp.

Back in the "pariah" room, they were still waiting for the waiter. The baby was trying to eat her father and Mike and Ruthie were down on the floor playing with the silverware. The rest of them were thirsty.

"You'd think he'd at least bring us some water," Katy complained. "Just some lousy old ice water." We explained about table water in Europe.

After some fifteen minutes, the baby now having joined the company on the floor, the waiter returned with his pad and his pencil poised over it. *"Bitte schön?* (Your order, please?)" he asked.

"What is *Hinterschenkelstück?"* asked my husband in German.

The waiter's mouth dropped open. *"Hinterschenkelstück —is Hinterschenkelstück!"* he explained, shrugging.

"Oh!" said Pete. "And what is— Oh, never mind. What have you? Something good! But not sauerkraut!"

The waiter smiled. He pointed to something on the menu.

"Bring it!" Pete said nodding.

"I don't want it!" Jean cried. "All I want is some toast and milk. Daddy, can't you say toast and milk in German?"

"Milk have we not on Sunday," said the waiter.

"Have you bread? Toasted bread?"

"Daddy, here's something that looks like bananas. It says

'Ananas,' " Helen said. "Can I have that?"

"Ananas! Oh yes! *Es ist obst*—fruit," said the waiter, writing.

"It *is* bananas! He says it's fruit! Daddy, I can understand German!"

"Okay," Pete said. "That's all! And coffee for the lady and me. And water for the children."

"Don't forget to say '*bitte*.' " I said, "*bitte*."

The waiter disappeared, to be replaced by the little blonde girl. She stood in the doorway, still holding the frightening can of baby food and looking as if she would cry. "*Bitte*." she kept saying, "*bitte*."

I hurried over to her, "It must warmed be. Make hot. In hot water. Water in pan. Make hot. Hot! But open first." I said in German. I made motions of opening with a can opener. "*Bitte!* Do you understand?" She nodded woefully and scurried away.

"Something good" turned out to be hot roast beef sandwiches with gravy, but "ananas" turned out to be canned pineapple, lots and lots of canned pineapple! The toast was hot and liberally buttered. The baby had toast, pineapple juice and gravy. Finally her can of liver and bacon arrived, smoking like Vesuvius. I must have said "hot" too many times.

We felt quite a lot more confident after dinner, and all repaired with great nonchalance to the *Herren* and *Damen*. My husband was informed that *all* the hotels in town were good and two across the street were pointed out.

The lobby of the first hotel looked promising. It was

warm, good-smelling, movie-like—those old movies where everybody waves steins and sings. The proprietor was fat with a sweeping mustache. But unfortunately they were full, he told us, eyeing the children warily. He advised us to try the hotel next to where we had parked our car just off the main square. It looked rather motheaten to us. Bleak. Uncaring. We didn't trust it. So we tried the one right next door. It had no lobby, just a tiny restaurant with a mahogany counter on which sat an immense brass beer-cooler, three small tables, all with checked tablecloths and shaded lights dangling over them.

Out of this cozy nest, a plump woman took us into a cold back hall smelling of hundreds of years of German cooking (with cabbage) and up an immense dark stairway into echoing caverns. The keys to our chambers were as big as teaspoons, with saucer-like brass plaques dangling from them.

If there hadn't been electric lights—with the wiring all visible on the walls, I'd have sworn we had passed into a time machine and would wake up the next morning to witness the coronation of Wilhelm the Second.

In all my life I have never seen such frightening rooms. The children were silent in awe and stood as close as they could get to me and their father. They were huge and high-ceilinged, with walls stained, veined and cracked in gloomy patterns. On them were ancient framed prints of bosomy ladies with dripping sleeves, sitting on benches in dark gardens contemplating birds or else looking down on a kneeling man with massive calves who was offering roses. There were enormous marble sinks and in the commodes beside the beds, chamber pots were invitingly displayed.

Ruthie caught her breath. "Mama," she cried, "look at the great big cup! Are there giants here?"

"I don't know," I said grimly, "I wouldn't be surprised at anything! But don't you worry. Mama will protect you!" I cast a dirty look at Pete when the woman departed. "You and your Kiel Canal!"

I was tired and near the point of tears. I didn't want to cry, so I got bad tempered. He was tired, too, since he had been driving all day, but he had the Kiel Canal to look forward to, after all. And the Kiel Canal was why we were here and not in wonderful Copenhagen, going to sleep in our own house.

The windows were hidden by two sets of draperies— lace and something else that had been woven before the flood. I pulled both sets and a great staring eye of rainy window which couldn't be budged open appeared. The furniture was dark, ornate and enormous. The children gingerly approached the beds which were the only fresh-looking objects in the rooms. These were made up with feather beds enveloped in sheeting. The mattresses seemed to be hinged and built up at the head ends.

In each room, two single beds were pushed together and there were two extra cots. The one where Jean, the seven-year-old, was to sleep was covered by a piece of tapestry-looking stuff which might once have wrapped a mummy. "Take it off—it scares me," Jean wailed. I folded it gingerly for fear it would crack and stuffed it in with a chamber pot.

We made our dreary journeys down the hall in relays

with the children. They were afraid of the toilet with the menacing tank set high above it and the chain dangling heavily, and then they were afraid of going to bed. They were terribly afraid of going to bed—not the older girls, Helen and Katy, of course—but the four youngest ones. It took us a long time to get them to sleep.

I was giddy from weariness.

"Let's go downstairs and see what's doing," Pete said, "and maybe have a cup of coffee." He was all for taking a walk in the rain, too, but I said I wouldn't leave the children alone in this nightmare for anything.

"Ah well," he said, when we were settled downstairs at a little table with our coffee trays before us, "it really isn't so bad, is it?"

"Not if there aren't bedbugs!" I answered.

The only other couple in the room got up, put on their coats and hats and left.

"I do believe we're the only people staying in this hotel," Pete said. "You haven't seen anybody else, have you?"

"Just the vampire and the fat man with the square head!"

"You're tired," he said. "A good night's rest and you'll be raring to go. Tomorrow," he promised, "we'll be crossing the Kiel Canal!"

"Well, it better be good!" I warned.

"You know," he said, smiling, "when I was a boy, I used to think about how some day I'd see the Kiel Canal. I don't know just why. It was something to do with Count von Luckner, the Sea Devil, and the Battle of Jutland or something. I don't quite remember the connection, but anyhow he was a great hero of mine—when I was in Junior High."

"When *I* was a girl," I put in, "back in Nathaniel Morton Junior High School in Plymouth, Mass., *I* used to dream of living in luxury in a Paris hotel! Breakfast in bed every morning, silk sheets, and a maid to scrub my back." I gave him a long level look. "You puzzle me. You really do. You know, a man who prides himself on being logical, a scientist, no less, shouldn't keep on saying 'I don't know just why! Something like that! I don't quite remember the connection. It tastes good but it isn't quite the same! Maybe you should burn the sugar a little more!'"

"Oh for heaven's sake!" he said. "Are we back on that again? Why can't women ever let a thing go?"

"What happened back at Onaway Junior High School, anyhow? What happened that casts glory on nothing but a big ditch like the Kiel Canal? Was it a girl?" I asked.

"Oh, stop that," he said. "You want any more coffee? Then let's go on up to bed. You're tired, dear. It's been a long day. We'll all feel better in the morning."

So I tottered beside him up the smelly stairs, entered our no-color room, and we undressed and got into bed as quickly as possible so as not to look at the walls any longer than we had to and so that morning could come sooner and with it—the Kiel Canal.

It was still raining in the morning. We ate downstairs, where the proprietress produced excellent breakfasts from a sordid little room behind the counter. Fortified with eggs and hot milk which the proprietress had bullied them into drinking, the children ran out on the town to see what they could do with a few marks. Pete and I bathed the baby, packed our bags and loaded them into the bus. The children came splashing up with pastries and candy, completely thrilled with Germany and bakeries!

"It's easy to buy things in Germany," Jean cried. "All you do is point at what you want and then hold out the money and they give you back the change."

"Everybody *loves* us," four-year-old Ruthie exclaimed, "they really do!"

"Boy, I like this place!" Mike said, biting into a bear claw, "only one thing, they don't have any bubble gum!"

My husband's eyes were bright, his color hearty. He hummed as we sizzled along in the rain, the drinking song from *The Student Prince*. He was obviously back in his dream world, clinking steins with that courtly daredevil, Count von Luckner, his second in a duel he'd just won over some little blonde in Onaway Junior High School.

I fumed. "Oh, is this the Kiel Canal?" I'd say. "Why, we have a bigger ditch than that in our back yard! The kids dug it yesterday to bury a hummingbird!" Or

"Oh, don't tell me *this* is the Kiel Canal," I'd say, "why it isn't nearly as big as the Cape Cod Canal! When we used to drive down on a summer's night to watch the New York boat go through! Back when I was in Nathaniel Morton Junior High School!"

"Drink! Drink! Drink!" Pete burst out suddenly, waving his stein.

"Oh, keep still!" I muttered.

23

"What's that you said, dear? I wasn't listening."

"I said I sure hope this rain clears up so you can get some good slides of the Kiel Canal."

"We ought to see it soon," he said. "Of course, the way we're going now, we aren't going to see it at its biggest. You understand—I don't want to go *too much* out of the way on this trip because I'm just as anxious to get to Copenhagen as you are. But when we come down here again, we can see it at the point where they have this big railroad bridge. That ought to be a thrilling sight. They only have three of these in the whole world. You see, the cars roll on to this sort of bridge thing and this is just lifted up and carried across, train and all! I want to get some slides of that sometime."

"You mean we'll be coming this way *again?*" I wailed.

"Probably be rattling back and forth across Schleswig-Holstein three or four times this year. After all, there's only one other way to drive out of Denmark. But we'll go that way, too!"

"Thanks," I said.

The rain let up in the middle of the morning; however, the skies remained gray. And then, at last, we were approaching the Kiel Canal. There was a tantalizing gleam of silver ahead as we topped a little hill; it disappeared as we rolled down.

"Of course, it doesn't look like much at this point," said Pete anxiously. There was nothing in sight but green meadows with cows grazing in them, a small cluster of tile-topped houses, a few trees, and a tall grassy dyke that stretched away into the grayness. From the car, I couldn't even see any water—certainly no ships.

"Is *this* it?" I screeched. "Is *this* the Kiel Canal? We came out of the way and stayed in that hotel to see this *nothing!* Why, it isn't even a respectable ditch!"

He didn't hear me. He pulled the car over to the side of the road just before we got to the bridge, reached for his camera silently, paused, looked out at the gray morning, and left the camera where it was. He got out of the car, not asking if we wanted to. For the moment we didn't exist for him. We watched him climb the embankment. He stood at the top for awhile, looked back at us, gave a jaunty little wave and trudged slowly farther off until he was just a gray silhouette in the mist. Then he stood motionless for what seemed a long, long time.

I stared at him, wondering, until my eyes fogged over and I was gripped by a sudden, almost unbearable, nostalgia. Because all at once I knew what he was seeing. I had seen it myself just three days before when our ship had anchored at Cobh, Ireland. There on a cliff, high above the town, were the ruins of a castle. And I had stood at the rail, gazing at it entranced—even as Pete was standing now— lost again in childhood and in its towering absolutes: the bravest of all brave knights, the most beautiful damsel in white samite and the simplest blackest evil witch overcome. This was before I knew that the knight picked lice from his seams, the white samite was gray with dirt and the evil witch was the product of an underprivileged childhood.

The children began to grumble.

"What's he standing there so long for?" Mike asked. "I can't see anything."

"What's so great about the Kiel Canal anyway?" Jean inquired.

"Now you keep still," I said unevenly. "Don't you say anything to your father when he comes back. Just be nice, all of you."

He came leaping down the embankment. His cheeks were flushed, his eyes bright. He cleared his throat as he got into the car.

"Of course, it doesn't look like so much at this point and in this weather!" He started the motor, and slowly, in reverent silence, we went up on the bridge and crossed the Kiel Canal.

# 3. THE ANTIQUE WORLD

LATE THAT AFTERNOON, SEPTEMBER 17, TWO DAYS BEFORE
Alice's first birthday, we crossed the border into Denmark.
Right away we felt at home. The roads were as good as
those in California, the dark forests fell away and the sky
opened up. Signposts were red and white, striped like sticks
of candy, and the farmhouses were many-windowed, every
window crowded with plants.

27

We spent the night at the Søgaardhus, a pleasant inn, well aired and spotless, furnished with charm and dash, where everybody spoke English. At dinner, there were flowers on the tables and pounds of butter lay casually about.

Our sense of well-being and complete satisfaction with Denmark lasted all the next day. But the children got restless during a long wait for the ferry from the island of Fünen to Zealand, and the hotel we chose in a hurry at Korsør was far from idyllic. We were put in a dark wing where we seemed to be the only occupants and had to walk up three flights to get to our rooms. The lights we put on downstairs went out before we'd made it upstairs.

Nothing worked in that hotel. Confidently I threw Alice's paper diaper into the hall toilet and pulled the chain. There was a hollow clunk. A little spit of water came down, disturbing the diaper not at all, and then a great sighing business went on in the tank four feet above my head. I tried again. Not even a spit of water. When we came back after dinner, the diaper was gone and the toilet clean. It worked for somebody, but it still refused to work for us.

There were sinks in each of our rooms, with taps marked V (*varm*) for hot and K (*kold*) for cold. But no hot water came out of the V, just K and precious little of that, and once it got into the basin, it didn't want to go down the drain. I spent most of the evening carrying glasses of water out to flush down the toilet.

Jean, our middle daughter, slept in an alcove just off our room. There was a door in the alcove and curious to see where it led, I turned the latch. It came off in my hand.

I collapsed laughing, gave up on everything and climbed into bed. Pete tried to close the window draperies and the whole arrangement fell on top of him.

At noon of the following day, we reached Copenhagen and fell in love with it immediately. After lunch at which we had a cake with one candle for Alice, we picked up our landlord's daughter and she drove with us the twenty miles north to Birkehave. This was the name of the house we had arranged to rent the July before from Herr Sagfører Lund, a lawyer in Copenhagen whose family used it as a summer place. (Sagfører means lawyer).

At that time, we could hardly believe our good fortune in obtaining so much living space for our outsize family in a country where there was a severe housing shortage. And modern conveniences, too! A refrigerator, for instance, an electric stove, a washing machine. And all for such paltry rent by American standards—one hundred and twenty-seven dollars per month. We were also offered the services of a "house assistant," Fru Svendsen, at thirty-five cents an hour. It was a miracle, no less.

Annelise Lund, the landlord's daughter, was a beautiful young woman of twenty-two who spoke perfect English with an Oxford accent. She was my ideal of womanhood, when I was thirteen or fourteen. In those days, I was going to be beautiful, of course, well-bred but sexy, tall yet not too tall, modest yet able to exhibit a command of history, literature, six modern languages and two ancient. Nobody but God could have achieved the reconciliation of opposites that I was going to manage, and I realized it after awhile. But that day in Copenhagen, Annelise appeared to have a fair start on it and I resented her.

The poor tired, little raggle-taggle family on arrival in Copenhagen, with their array of sad baggage, were met by a kind, beautiful, rich young lady and escorted to her mansion in the country, I told myself as I sat in the back of the Volkswagen with the children crawling all over me, while up in front Annelise graciously pointed out the way to my dazzled husband.

She told us that her father and mother were enjoying a little vacation in Sweden, but that they would return Sunday and Herr Lund would visit us on the Monday to make sure that we were comfortable and all was in order.

If I stood in awe of Annelise, nothing can describe my fright when we arrived at Birkehave and drove up the long curving drive to the house. It was set on the crest of a hill and from it descended velvet lawns and careful gardens, the whole fringed with rhododendrons and trees. We piled out of the bus and gawked, then circled the house warily while Annelise went inside to help Fru Svendsen prepare tea for us. From the back, at the bottom of the hill, it reared up four stories, looking like a ship on the crest of a green wave, ready to sweep over us and flatten us under a load of sparkling windows and floors. Wistfully I looked down at the spread of small tiled roofs, the modest houses and yards fringing our erstwhile estate. I was going to be queen of the hill and I had already begun to fret under the burden.

Early on Monday morning, five days after our arrival,

my husband prepared to take the three older children to school. Arrangements had been made the Friday before for Helen and Katy to be enrolled in the Mellemskole, the equivalent of our junior high, and for Jean to go to elementary school. We had even managed to find a private kindergarten for Mike and Ruthie, but they could not be admitted until the first of October, a week hence.

The three girls were in the bus, with lunch bags and new briefcases and I was standing in the doorway, holding the baby and listening to last minute instructions from my husband. Inside, the floors no longer sparkled, the breakfast dishes waited on the table, the beds were unmade and dirty clothes lay about the floor. My husband had just informed me that after he had deposited the girls at school, he would run along into Copenhagen to the University.

"Got to get started sometime," he said, impatiently.

"You mean you're going to leave me here in all this mess to talk to Herr Lund *alone?*"

"Fru Svendsen will be coming along at ten," he said, "and she'll clean things up. You've got to stop being so scared of the Lunds. So what if the house *is* a mess! You can't move into any place with six kids and spend two or three days out shopping just to get enough stuff so you can live in this completely furnished house. *Completely furnished!* By God, honey, learn to look at things from *our* point of view! I can't see where we owe Lund a damn thing! Where else is he going to get somebody to take care of his house during the winter and make him pay to do it."

"Daddy," Helen called from the car, "we're already late.

Aren't you ever coming?"

"Oh, go on," I sighed, "don't start *that* all over again!"

"Well, you'll be all right," he said, "and when Herr Lund comes, give him the money for the fuel oil, the whole ninety bucks worth! I left it in the desk. And ask him where *his* land stops and ours begins. And *don't* forget to mention that iron cord!"

"You mean I have to start right off with complaints?"

"Listen," he said, "it isn't a complaint—it's a legitimate request. With what we're paying for this place," he sighed, "and with what it's going to cost us before we're through, he can't possibly quibble over a lousy little iron cord!"

I watched the car go down the drive and then turned reluctantly back into the house. We were both more than a little disgruntled. The estate had already begun its process of diminution, and so, alas, had our funds. The vast fuel tank buried outside the house had just swallowed up ninety dollars worth of oil. The grounds, we discovered, were maintained by a gardener. We would have to pay him only for keeping up "our" part of them. How much "our" part was, we did not yet know, but he'd spent all day Saturday working. One of the two garages and certain rooms in the basement also were reserved for the Lunds.

And we had already in various ways "lost" three rooms, the living room, the reception hall and Mike's bedroom.

The living room formed a wing off by itself, exposed there on the hill to the elements, with large, loose windows on three sides. Obviously it would be difficult to heat, once the winter settled down upon us. As it was, *any* use of the

living room, whatever the season, seemed doubtful. The
furniture looked stunning, but it was unusable, at least from
our point of view. There was an antique stand-up desk
which through the centuries had been touched only by
gentle people wearing gloves. There was a short sofa with
a narrow seat which forbade any but the most rigid posture,
and this was flanked by antique cabinets openable by tiny
keys, just the sort that little girls love to wear on strings
around their necks. An inlaid table or two, a frail oriental,
a few Louis XIV armchairs, and a gleaming grand piano
completed the furnishings.

In the reception hall, the floor was made of polished
blocks of stone which shone like a rink of black ice, fairly
begging for a game of hockey. The blue porcelain stove was
encrusted with a number of fragile golden curlicues, the
walls bore plates of antique Meissen, and delicate chairs were
set precisely around them. There was a stern high-backed
love seat. Naturally, the little children wanted to spend
their days sliding across the floor, banging into the stove
and chairs and jarring the Meissen. It was clear we could
seldom use the reception hall.

All grandeur ceased at the French doors which separated
the reception hall from the dining room. Once the hand-
woven cloth was removed from the dining room table,
rough weatherbeaten planks with half-inch interstices set
upon scurfy once-gilded legs were revealed. The chair
seats were protected by plastic covers, and the veneer was
peeling off in places on the bird's-eye maple sideboard.
There was no other furniture in this enormous room save

a *small* side table.

The kitchen was tiny, with no space for eating. Its sole pride was the waist-high refrigerator. There were three beat-up pots and a frying pan very thin on half its circumference. It did not take long to discover why. The right burner of the two-burner electric stove, the one with controls—the other burner put forth only enough heat to maintain a slow simmer—burnt everything in front and was lukewarm in back. Other kitchen aids consisted of two wooden spoons and two teaspoons, two sets of butter-ball paddles, a spatula, three worn knives, a beat-up set of scales and weights, a partly unsprung wire whisk, a small legless ironing board which had to be used on a counter, and an iron with a badly frayed cord. We had spent two days in the stores supplementing the kitchen equipment and the bedding, but my husband had bogged down on buying a new cord for the iron.

"We rented a furnished house, by God," he said, "*complete* except for silver, linens and part of the bedding. Now I can't quibble about a definition of 'complete,' and I suppose you could get along, if you had to, with this junk. And if there weren't any iron at all, I couldn't argue—we'd just buy one and say nothing. But there *is* an iron, by God, such as it is—" he banged the counter so that the iron jumped, "and the damn thing's unusable! Look at that," he said disgustedly, running the cord through his fingers. "The wire's exposed in four or five different places. It's downright dangerous. And I'm damned if *I'll* buy a new one!"

If he's damned if he'll buy a new one, he could at least tell Herr Lund, himself, I thought.

I set the baby down on the floor and, for the fifth time that morning, shooed Mike and Ruthie out of the reception hall where they had been merrily sliding across the rink. I picked up two handfuls of breakfast dishes, took them into the kitchen and found the baby had crawled half way up the precipitous back stairs. I ran up to save her, took her the rest of the way upstairs and wandered aimlessly about, holding her in my arms.

The third floor was cut up into five bedrooms, a dressing-room, two baths and two halls with an intricate system of leading one into the other, so that I still was not sure each time I opened a door in what room I'd find myself.

Up here, we had lost the other room, the one we'd intended for Mike. It was small, not much more than a passage from the front hall to the back hall, and it contained no furniture except a bed. But at last, we thought, our boy could have a little place to himself. He was so tired the first night that he dropped off to sleep immediately. But the next night, we had no sooner tucked him in bed and got half-way downstairs than we heard shrieks from his room that sounded as if he were about to be murdered.

The walls of the room were red and there was a picture, on the one that faced his bed, of two pixies with pointed ears and floating hair which were innocuous enough in the daytime, but when the light was turned off that night, the moonlight had cast flickering tree shadows on the bloody walls, making them look like the flames of hell and the pixies were transformed into batlike creatures with huge white faces.

We took the picture from the wall and tried to coax Mike to go to sleep, but he said he could still see the bats and clung to us, moaning piteously. He spent the rest of that night in Ruthie's bed and, after a futile struggle the next night and the night after that, we knew we wouldn't be able to pry him out for the rest of the year. Nobody else would sleep in the room either, since there was no closet for the older girls' dresses, and Mike had infected Ruthie and Jean with his terrors. The baby slept in the dressing room off the master bedroom. We had rented a crib for her. Helen and Jean shared a room and a bed, and Katy slept in solitary splendor in the maid's room off the back stairs.

Downstairs, once again, still holding Alice, I decided I was no good for any work that day. I would just let Fru Svendsen worry about the mess. I was hoping she would arrive before Herr Lund so that she could offer me moral support. For I had immediately sensed in her a friend and ally. There was nothing hidden in her face; no sly taking of my measure when we met. When I had greeted her in Danish on the day of our arrival, her face had broken into a broad grin.

"Ah, you speak Danish," she had exclaimed, shaking hands all over again.

"Only a little," I replied.

"Well, I will teach you," she promised. "I come Monday, Wednesday and Friday at eight. Is that all right? But next Monday, I come a little late. I have a big party to help with the night before."

So on that Monday, Herr Lund arrived first at the front door. I had just put jackets on Mike and Ruthie and sent them out back to play in the orchard. Herr Lund was a precise man of fifty, wearing a black overcoat with a mink collar and immaculate gloves. His mouth was thin and tight. His hair was blond with a painful part and lay as hard across his head as if it had been stuck there with glue.

He apologized for not having been in town when we arrived, removed his gloves and shook hands with me and Alice. This is the first thing you learn in Denmark—you shake hands all around.

He seemed not to notice the scratches on the black stone floor nor the smudged condition of the parquet in the dining room.

"Is everything all right?" he asked in careful English. "You have everything you need? You are comfortable? You must tell me if there is anything wrong."

"Everything is just perfect!" I gushed. "This is *such* a beautiful place, and your daughter was *so* kind, showing us around, serving us tea and everything!"

"Not at all, not at all! I am so glad! And there is nothing further I can do for you?"

"Well, I almost hate to mention it," I ventured, made bold by his solicitude.

"Oh no! You *must* tell me!"

"It's such a little thing—"

"I *beg* of you, tell me!"

"Well, all right," I said, taking a long breath. Setting Alice

37

down on the dining room floor, I led the way to the kitchen.

"It's the cord on this iron. It's dreadfully frayed, right down to the wires, and we're scared it might cause a fire. Do you suppose we could have a new one?"

His smile vanished. Blank of face, he took the cord into his manicured hands as if it were something precious and examined it at great length.

"Hmmmmm," he said. "Hmmmmmm. Yes. But I don't think you *really* need a new one, do you? Now, you see, you will just get some tape and wind it around these few places, and then it will be as good as new, hmmmmm?" He turned his examining gaze at me and I felt as if he'd delivered me a blow in the stomach.

But I persisted. "Well, maybe you have some tape, then?"

"Oh no! But you can get it, I'm sure, in any electrical store."

"I see," I said. "Well, thanks anyway." We stared at each other for a moment, piercing each other's depths. He hit jelly. I hit stone. Then we began to smile formally and walked back to the dining room, where I handed him his ninety dollars, his six hundred and thirty *kroner*, for the fuel oil.

Merry shouts were coming from the apple orchard through the partly opened window. We looked out. Mike and Ruthie were up in a tree, picking apples and flinging them down.

"That reminds me," he said, tucking the *kroner* in his bulging wallet, "we, my family and I, plan to come out over the weekend and pick our apples on that little property down there we reserve for our own use. And now, I must take my leave."

He offered me his hand before drawing on his gloves. "And please, if there is *anything* at all, *any* small thing—you understand?"

"I understand," I told him as we arrived at the front door. "*Farvel.*" At least, I could show him I knew a word or two of Danish!

I watched him from the window as he cut across the lawn toward the front garden, removed a pen knife from his pocket and began to cut a bouquet of what I had, up until that moment, thought of as *my* asters.

"Damn!" I said, stamping my foot. "Damn!" And then in a fury, I tore out the back door, into the orchard and pulled the children out of the trees.

"What's the matter, Mommy?" Mike asked. "Why are you so mad?"

"I'm mad because this isn't our orchard," I told him, "and those aren't our flowers in front! And I'm sick and tired! Wait until that—that *man* goes away, and then you can play out front in the gravel! I *think* it's our *gravel*, anyway."

After I had got the three children settled playing with cans in the driveway, I went in for a much-needed cup of coffee. I sat down with it at the dining room table, shoving aside the dirty dishes. It was not yet ten o'clock and I was weary to the bone. Beyond the French doors, now smudgy with finger marks, the reception hall glittered, quite the perfect place for Louis XIV to hold his levée. And then that ghostly company could step into the Salle Pleyel next door and sit up straight, tall, and freezing, while it listened to Chopin playing his preludes—wearing fur-lined gloves, of course! Balzac might tear off a chapter or two at the stand-up desk before he got frostbitten. But for *live* people like us, with flesh and bones, the place was a total loss. There wasn't one piece of comfortable furniture, not a full-length sofa in the place on which to sprawl in the evening and read. We were paying for three thousand square feet of living space and half of it we couldn't use. We were paying a gardener to take care of the yard, and the landlord was picking the flowers!

I stared listlessly out of the window where my baby could be seen crawling speedily down the drive and Mike and Ruthie pitching cans full of gravel onto the lawn where next Saturday it would ruin the power mower.

Well, let it, I thought, and let old Pinchpenny pay for it! After which I reflected that it would naturally be ourselves who paid and got up with a sigh.

And then, pedalling up the drive, her net bag draped over her cycle basket, came the *dea ex machina*. She got off the machine, propped it against the house and picked up the baby; she made Mike and Ruthie understand that they must pitch the gravel back onto the drive; and in a minute she was coming in the door with a cheerful "God dag."


At the end of the week, I was a much happier woman. I had picked up from Fru Svendsen a couple of phrases of vulgar Danish, "Det gør ikke noget!" ("it doesn't matter") to see me through any minor difficulty, and "Skidt med den!" (roughly translated, "the hell with it!") for a real crisis. And I had learned from her that Herr Lund was a creature called a Swede who was stiff and didn't do things like you and me. Also, he took care of his money! This last was told me with a wink, a squeezing motion of the hand and a shrug.

The house somehow had become much more livable. Fru Svendsen had found a gate which she fastened with twine across the bottom step of the back stairway so that Alice couldn't climb up any more. And we had brought down from the second floor two shabby but quite comfortable brown velour chairs and a table on which to set the one reading lamp in the house. We grouped these by the radiator in the dining room.

Time such as I had never before known, luxurious time, stretched before me in the long afternoons when the children took their naps and I read, warm and comfortable in my chair, the house clean, the wash done. The telephone never rang, no one came selling magazine subscriptions, no jets cracked the sound barrier and set the windows to rattling. And in a house of mine, for the first time, there were two rooms always in perfect order in case the King and Queen came to visit.

The very first afternoon, the children had come home bringing friends with them. Helen brought Lene, Katy brought Birgit, and Jean arrived half an hour later with Kathy whose mother was Scotch and who was the only girl in her class who could speak a little English. All of them were obviously impressed by the house on the hill.

After we had been introduced and had shaken hands, I asked, "Well, how was school?"

Helen groaned. "*Mother*, it was murder! Here we were out in the yard, having lunch, and *everybody* was staring at us. And we had to reach in our paper bags and bring out our Dagwoods and a whole big pickle! *They* were all eating these little dainty *smørrebrøds* out of aluminum cases. We just died! We'll have to get some of that real thin rye bread and wholewheat bread, *rugbrød* and *fullkornsbrød*, is that right?" she turned questioning to Lene, "and then you put a little slice of sausage or cheese on it and that's all. But, Ma, one boy had mashed potatoes spread on his!" She giggled. Lene and Birgit had not understood all this conversation but stood smiling politely, two tall blonde girls with rosy cheeks, wearing neat windbreakers, plaid skirts and long navy-blue cotton stockings.

"And Ma," Katy broke in, "can I get some stockings like that? Nobody in school wears ankle socks."

"Come on, Lene and Birgit, and we'll show you the rest of the house." Off they dashed. I heard them say as they stared at the wonders of the two front rooms, "Eeeee, hvor det er fint!" ("How fine it is!")

Then the French doors were respectfully closed. They retreated to the kitchen for apples and milk, talking in a babble of Danish and English, punctuated by giggles. One of the girls asked, "Skal vi ud?" ("Shall we out?") and they all ran outside to play *hinklesten*, a form of hopskotch.

At the end of the next week, you couldn't tell the older girls from Danes. Helen had changed her sprawling American writing for a neat German script and, when she didn't forget, she spoke English with a Danish accent. They both had Danish haircuts and had acquired duvetyn jackets and plaid slacks. Almost every day the principal of the school gave them a half hour lesson in Danish. He told us they would be speaking it fluently before Christmas.

Mike and Ruthie had started kindergarten. They left each morning at quarter to nine, carrying knapsacks which held their lunches and school slippers. All children had to change from their boots, street shoes or *traesko*—leather-topped shoes with wooden soles—into slippers. Wooden shoes make a terrible noise in the house, we soon found out.

The baby had begun to walk. She toddled about the house after Fru Svendsen and learned, among other things, what Danish animals say.

"What does the dog say?" Fru Svendsen would ask. To which Alice replied,

"Vov-vov."

Danish cows say "Buuu—buuuuu," and Danish roosters say "Kyrkliki."

My husband had settled down to work at the lab after his colleagues had treated him to several convivial tours of Copenhagen. He knew his way around the city. And he had discovered the bust of Sophus Schandorf.

Sophus was a writer and member of a commission to Germany in the nineteenth century. He must have been a spectacular failure, to judge from his bust which sat on a pedestal in Øster Anleg, a park Pete crossed daily on his way from the train station to the lab. One look at Sophus and all your troubles slipped off like water from a duck's back at the sight of his utter, abject misery. There was usually a bird perched on his head and bird droppings had dripped all over his face, making him weep quantities of large white tears.

"What was the use of it all?" he seemed to be asking, "when I can't even keep these birds off my head!"

"I spend a minute with Sophus and I'm set up for the day," said my husband. "He's better than a cold shower!"

Meanwhile I was learning Danish cooking. One day Fru Svendsen brought me a large red cabbage and a bottle of homemade *saft*, which is a sort of thin fruit jelly, and taught me how to make *rødkaal*, an accompaniment to roast pork or duck. I also learned how to make applecake by combining cold applesauce with bread crumbs, this to be eaten with quantities of whipped cream, and how to fry potatoes with a little sugar so that they brown nicely, and save the margarine. (Margarine was cheap, but Fru Svendsen was thrifty.) She could never sell me on beer soup, however. I would not make it, although she told me that it would be very strengthening for Alice. King Christian ate a big bowl of beer soup every day of his life and urged all Danes to do the same. Beer soup is made of rye bread first soaked and then cooked into a porridge with white ale and spices and is eaten with sugar and cream. It sounded revolting to me, and I successfully avoided even tasting it.

So we caught on to life in Denmark and rode it happily enough. The golden days of October faded into a darkening

November and we had seen very little of the Lunds since that first Sunday when they had come out to pick the apples. There were six of them in the family. There were two boys and two girls: Annelise, twenty-two; Christian, nineteen, who wore his blonde hair in a bang like Truman Capote; Tove, nine; and Henning, six. They were handsome children, the two little ones very well behaved. They had brought a picnic hamper from the city, and they ate their lunch in the rooms downstairs which I had never seen.

They picked the apples in the afternoon, making a game of it. The males climbed the trees and handed the apples down carefully to the females who stored them in boxes. There was much laughter and chatter, and it was quite apparent that they loved one another dearly. We watched them from the dining room window.

"Marie Antoinette and members of her court playing peasant," I said.

"You can be nasty at times, can't you?" asked my husband.

"What *is* it about them that irritates me so? I keep thinking he doesn't ever take his coat off—even when he goes to bed. They seem to be on stage all the time. I think they're a bunch of phonies."

"Oh, come on," he said.

"I don't like myself when I talk to them. I show off—all big words and superlatives. Perfectly lovely! Utterly charming! And a false smile pasted all over my face."

"Well, that isn't *their* fault," he said.

"You weren't so happy yourself a few days ago, about the

iron cord and the difference in furnishings between the front of the house and the back."

"That's all in the past now. So, he's a little 'near,' as Fru Svendsen says. So are lots of people. Some very rich people save string. Is that any reason to pick them to pieces?"

At the end of the apple picking, the Lunds stored all the boxes but one in *their* garage, where they also kept the power lawnmower. Then they knocked at the back door.

Herr Lund asked Pete if he would mind bringing in the box of apples to their apartment in town the next day since it would be a little heavy for them to take on the train. He didn't realize Pete usually took the train to Copenhagen instead of driving. Pete said he would be glad to.

"But first," said Herr Lund, to me, "you must take out some apples for yourself, as many as you like."

"See?" I said to my husband as soon as the door was closed and they were merrily on their way down the drive with their picnic hamper swinging between Annelise and Christian. "Now, he could just as well have put some apples in a paper bag or a box. I can't stand people like that. I'll bet he's put all the crummy ones on top, too."

"Don't be so petty!"

"Who's petty? Do you know they have a big stand-up ironing board downstairs that they keep for when they're here over the weekend, and I have to iron *dresses* on that thing that sits on the counter? Now, I ask you, how in the world could I ruin an ironing board?"

"Search me," he said. "Maybe it's made of inlaid mahogany."

I giggled. "No, it isn't. I saw it and it's just an ordinary ironing board. Friday I was ironing on *that* thing and Fru Svendsen said 'Skidt med den!' ('To hell with that!') and went downstairs in their quarters and brought theirs up. So I finished ironing on it. I was very careful not to scorch it!"

The next night my husband came home from Copenhagen with a play pen, a potty chair and a baby's crib that the Lunds thought we might be able to use.

"In return," said Pete, "he would like the bed from Mike's room since we don't use it. He needs it for Henning who's outgrown the crib."

"How does he *know* we don't use that bed?" I cried. "Don't tell me they've been romping around in here when we've been out!"

My husband shrugged. "Maybe Fru Svendsen told them. Anyway, I hope you'll have your chance to see how the other half lives. If you were flabbergasted by this place, wait'll you see their apartment in Copenhagen."

I couldn't help thinking, here we go again, losing some more of the house! We had given up a bed for the crib, which seemed like an even exchange. But we had also returned the crib we had rented and now we had a completely empty room upstairs.

"Well, we don't use the bed anyhow," said Pete. "And if you're so worried about having an empty room, we can just move Alice and the crib in there."

"But suppose we have company? No extra bed. And if we move the crib in there, then that leaves the dressing room empty. We're paying rent for empty space!"

"Well, they *meant* to be nice," he said. "They sent along the play pen and the potty chair."

"We've never had a kid yet that would stay in a play pen. And Alice won't use that potty chair until she's good and ready. Probably never!"

"*They* don't know that. Other kids use play pens and potty chairs!"

"Our kids don't."

"How would *they* know our kids are backward."

"They aren't backward—they're just independent."

"What a warhorse you've turned out to be!" he said.


It was the middle of November when I got my chance to see how the other half lived. We were invited by the Lunds for bridge and supper.

They lived in a ten-room apartment in the business district of Copenhagen. Many of the flats in the building had already been made into offices, but the Lunds hated to find another apartment; theirs was convenient to everything—the stores, the theaters, transportation—and the rent was cheap. Across the front of the apartment there were three enormous salons —I don't know what else to call them—opening into each other by means of double doors. Oriental rugs lay thick on the floors, overlapping each other. In silver candlesticks on tables ranged around the wall dozens of candles were burning, gleaming on pound after pound of other silver objects: antique pitchers, goblets, tankards, cups, plates, bowls, and even a belt made out of thin engraved silver medallions which, we were told, were seven hundred years old. The furniture was ornate and upholstered in velvet. Besides money and silverware, Herr Lund collected antique china and clocks. All the clocks were running and although it was not at all hot, I simmered in that room.

For awhile we sat and talked about television, the decline of culture in America and the rampant materialism there. Herr Lund dominated the conversation. He read *Time* magazine every week, so he was remarkably *au courant* on America. But plainly he didn't care much about it—the place was so crass and so vulgarly new. I had an urge to tell our hosts that we had the most remarkable antique in the world in the United States, the General Sherman tree in Sequoia National Park, but that wouldn't have impressed Herr Lund. He couldn't buy it and, besides, it was alive.

We repaired after awhile to an inlaid card table and played bridge. Around nine, we were escorted to the dining room for a repast, consisting of beef smørrebrød, different kinds of delicious breads and cheeses, cookies, little cakes filled with a chocolate butter mixture, and tea in fragile cups, after which we went back to the inlaid table and played more bridge and were offered Simon Artz cigarettes from a silver box.

That night as we drove home through the quiet streets of Copenhagen and over the still parkway past fields and farms, I began to think with longing of my own country, of its deserts and prairies empty of everything but the wind, of mountains made of rock and sand, and a vast lonely sky. And then I remembered Joe Shoshone.

I hadn't thought of him for a long time. One night in Death Valley five years before, Pete and I were sitting on the patio of Furnace Creek Ranch, talking with a man from the borax company. He told us about the old Indian born the year the Forty-niners came through, who had lived all his life in the valley and who came to the ranch every morning for pie and coffee. We got up early the next day so as not to miss seeing him. He came hobbling in on crutches and then sat sipping his coffee and eating his pie, looking out at the desert. His face was nothing but deep, hard wrinkles, a bony shaft of nose and steady black eyes peering out. Staring at him, I thought how he must have lived through most of his one hundred and two years, possessing nothing, feeding on snakes and lizards, trapped in that caldron by mountains and hostile tribes, the very least of humankind. And yet there he was—content.

By the time we got home to Birkehave, I was all the way back from Joe Shoshone, but I had lost a lot of my rancor toward Herr Lund and his family and some of my own complacency. True, I didn't need as *much* as Herr Lund did to make me happy. But Joe Shoshone put us both to shame.

So when Herr Lund sent men to take away the piano and leave in its place another tortured love seat, I shrugged my shoulders. Det gør ikke noget! I told myself, we don't use the piano anyway.

And even when Fru Svendsen came in one Wednesday morning, excited and eager to tell me the news she had heard from the Lund's maid the day before, that Herr Lund had bought a huge magnificent villa, Lykkebo, with untold hectares of ground and was putting Birkehave on the market, I maintained my calm.

Of course, we were bothered by prospective buyers the rest of the year. And bit by bit, during the spring, our furniture was taken away to be renovated for furnishing the two cottages on the new estate. We didn't care so much about the coffee table nor the blue and white curtains in Helen's bedroom, but the night Pete and I came back from a trip to England, picked up the children at Fru Svendsen's house and returned to Birkehave to find that, in our absence, Herr Lund had taken away the mattress from my husband's bed, I will admit we lost our insouciance. All night long, as we lay squeezed into my single, playing tug-of-war with the feather bed, I would wake from short dozes to hear my husband making uncomplimentary remarks about our landlord. The mattress was returned the next day with profuse apologies. It had taken longer to get it repaired than Herr Lund had thought.

The day finally came when the Lunds moved into Lykkebo. It took them a week. Fru Svendsen helped them and reported she had arranged whole shopsful of monogrammed linen on its shelves and services of china she thought only kings possessed. It was a month before they got settled. They had to have draperies made, the walls painted, the floors carpeted, and fifty keys chromium-plated. But one evening in the spring we drove over for supper. The villa even had its own street, a gate-keeper's cottage at the end of it, and the drive up to the main house was five times longer and curvier than Birkehave's. There were greenhouses and groves of trees; there was a little lake with a bad-tempered swan sailing over it; there was a terrace overlooking the lake on which a hundred people could be served tea. The living room was far too fine for anyone to sit in for very long, so after dinner we played bridge in a wide hall which extended the length of the house.

As we were about to leave, Herr Lund presented me with a plate one hundred years old, the first to be made in the pattern of china we had selected in Royal Copenhagen, and he said,

"It has not been such a good time for you here this year, I think."

"Oh, but it has," I told him. "In spite of everything we've enjoyed living in Birkehave. We loved the whole year."

"But so many annoyances—" he said.

"Yes," I admitted, "but I guess you have *those* everywhere!"

# 4. H. C. ANDERSEN
# IN THE WINTERTIME

AT BIRKEHAVE WE HAD A WILD RABBIT WHO SUNNED HIMSELF
at noon behind a clump of lilies. We had a family of red mice
in the woodpile and as Fru Svendsen and I ate our lunch, we
often watched them vying with the birds for the bread crusts
we'd set out.

Down in the cellar, we had *vaskmaskinen*, the electric
washing-machine, and its awesome companion, the hydro-

wringer. *Vaskmaskinen* was really a clothes boiler. You filled it with a hose, put in your wash and soap, plugged it in and then did other things for an hour or so until billows of soapy steam came upstairs after you. You fought your way down blindly and set a board with a paddle attached to its underside on top of *vaskmaskinen* and plugged *that* in. The paddle agitated the top layer of clothes, and although it sounded as if it would surely break down, it never did. After the clothes had cooked for twenty minutes, you took a pole and transferred them to the wringer, a heavy iron tub with a rubber bag hanging limp inside it.

Then you closed the lid, bolted it and turned on the cold water full force to run in between the tub and bag. Soapy water was thus squeezed out to gush over the floor—and incidentally your feet—and eventually to run into a drain under the set tubs. Then, of course, the clothes had to be rinsed and the wringing business repeated. Luckily Fru Svendsen usually did the washing. The few times I tried it, I got the best steam bath in Denmark.

We had lime trees in front of our house and on the lawn a clump of birches which gave it its name, "Birchgarden." We had nightingales.

But we had no television set. At first we didn't miss television a bit, even when, in November, night began to close down at four o'clock. After dinner we lingered at the table until it was time to put the younger children to bed. There was much to talk about.

Strange things happened at junior high school. The Carlsberg beer truck made weekly deliveries there. The teachers smoked during classes. In Helen's and Katy's English courses, their classmates were beginning to speak with American accents, contradicting the teacher's Oxford. One morning, Katy told us, she had called the principal *du*, the familiar form for "you," and sent the class into hysterics.

Jean was making progress in the second grade. She recited the multiplication tables in Danish for us. She had begun to read with the class from *Min Blaa Bog* (*My Blue Book*) instead of sitting all day reading Hans Christian Andersen in English.

Sometimes we talked about renting a television set, but it didn't seem worthwhile. At that time, Danish television functioned only two hours an evening and for that we weren't about to spend ten precious dollars a month. We were already renting a radio. We could listen to old American quiz shows on the Armed Forces program, American popular songs sung in Danish and Swedish and, if we were lucky, we could get the BBC Third Program and hear lectures on old English folk tunes.

November passed and there was Christmas to plan for. The children made paper chains to decorate the dining room and got busy with Christmas lists. There were real candles on our Christmas tree and we shot off firecrackers on New Year's Eve. So for four months, we were an ideal American family, an example of togetherness, even without a television set.

Then came the evening of Hans Christian Andersen.

Sooner or later in Denmark, you get around to Hans Christian Andersen, always referred to by the Danes as

H. C. Andersen. And when you do, it marks the end of something.

You are, for instance, out for dinner with your husband at the Store Kro, a charming inn at Hillerød. A lone Dane at the next table smiles, addresses you in English and soon you are having a conversation. After dessert, the three of you move out into the lobby and drink coffee and cognac together. He tells you of his visits to cities in the United States which you have never visited, and you mention places you have seen in Denmark which he has never seen. Then he deplores the high taxes in Denmark. He is a business man. You discuss American novelists and thus proceed naturally to a comparison of sex in the United States and Denmark. This calls for more coffee with cognac, and then you tell each other jokes. After a while you can't think of any more jokes, you begin to smother yawns, and H. C. Andersen comes up. So you know it's time to say farewell and go home.

Or you are at dinner at a friend's house. There are martinis in your honor to begin with. Then to the table for shrimps on bread and butter with gold label beer, ham, veal and mushrooms with white wine, and apple cake with marsala, after which you all arise from a final *skaal* and go into the living room for coffee and brandy. Later there are highballs and comparison of American and Danish dating customs and finally, to top it all off properly, openface sandwiches with beer or tea, and jokes. Then somebody mentions H. C. Andersen, everybody's eyes glaze, and the party breaks up.

Or you are reading one noon, while eating lunch. The

baby is asleep, it is warm and peaceful, and smells pleasantly of yesterday's bone-waxing. The back door bell rings, you answer, and there stands a very black boy with blue eyes and blonde hair. He tells you he wants to go up on the roof, you nod in a daze, and only when he has disappeared do you understand that he must be a chimney sweeper's apprentice. The chimney sweeper then appears, and *he* wants to go down cellar. You accompany him. He takes a black book from the top of the heater, writes in it, then opens a little door in the wall. After that, he relaxes, folds his arms—his hands are like black patent leather—and asks where in America you are from. You say California, which he interprets as Paradise and begins excitedly to question you. Between trying to understand his Danish and wondering how he ever gets clean, you become glassy-eyed. He laughs.

"Didn't you ever see a chimney sweep before?" he asks. "How do they get their chimneys cleaned in America?"

You never thought of this before. It leaves you speechless, especially in Danish.

"Ah," he laughs, "you didn't think we were real! You thought we were only in the fairy tales of H. C. Andersen."

With that, there is a fearsome scraping noise in the chimney, several loud plops, and vast clouds of soot emerge from the little door and set you to coughing uncontrollably.

Helen and I didn't get along very well that year. We might have got along better if I hadn't had so many books on child care around while she was growing up. She had read them

57

and knew exactly what she was supposed to be like at any given period. At fourteen, it seems, you do not get along with your mother.

Her girl friends in Denmark, all of whom seemed to be named Lene, Lone, or Lise, didn't get along very well with their mothers, either. They have these books in Denmark, too.

Occasionally I'd hear them talking about me. "My mother is very stubborn," Helen would say. "But the worst of all, she keeps telling me *my* memory is bad when it's *her* memory that's bad!"

I'd clench my teeth and think, Boy! When I get her alone! Then I'd try to relax and laugh about it. But things were going sour on me.

The three older girls set off to school each morning on their bicycles in the dark and came home in twilight. We turned on the heat in the bedrooms only at bedtime, and so we were all cooped together in the dining room from four o'clock on.

About once a week I went into Copenhagen to shop, visit the American library and have lunch or tea with Pete and stare at the matrons smoking their cigars. These were red letter days and refreshed me considerably.

And days when Fru Svendsen came passed quickly. She told me about her other jobs, at a Copenhagen doctor's house, and at our landlord's city apartment. She told me about her youth in Lolland, of waiting for the old king to come by on his morning walk and greet the children sitting on the fence, of the Polish immigrant girls employed on her father's farm. She told me about the day she stood by the main road from Helsingør and, with others, watched the defeated Germans march past to the border. They were only boys and she felt sorry for them, yet she spit at them and would not offer them water. And now that Jens, her own son was attaining that age, she often thought back to that day. Once she told me about castrating a boar. She was often vulgar but, somehow, always wholesome.

On days she didn't come, all I had to do was wash the dishes and make the beds. I might take the baby out for a walk to the village or play with her outside if it wasn't too dreary, but then she would go up for her long nap and I would find myself alone in the big-windowed house, whether reading or writing, conscious always of that pale sun outside, dragging itself miserably through the black treetops.

The grass was brown, the birds had flown. There was little snow that winter. The Eskimos know what to do in the dark. They dig themselves into the snow and create a world of heat and closeness. And the Scandinavians commit suicide or travel to Italy or go to drink coffee with their mothers.

In the dark afternoon the children came home.

"What's for dinner?" they'd ask. "Oh no, not fish again!" Or cabbage. Or brussels sprouts. Or applesauce. "Can't we ever have salad?"

"Stop complaining!" I'd snap. "Let's see *you* do the shopping. *You* find some lettuce and tomatoes."

And after dinner, there was not so much to talk about. We were all used to the teachers smoking, and nobody was corny enough to say *du* to principals anymore.

It is only when you exhaust small talk that you turn to philosophical discussion. And in philosophical discussion, somebody or everybody ends up with hurt feelings.

The evening of H. C. Andersen probably started off badly anyway—with codfish and kale and applesauce, to boot. With the coffee a discussion got underway. I can't remember exactly what it was all about, but Helen and I began to disagree, quite politely at first. It was I who first referred to H. C. Andersen in connection with it.

"It's just like *The Emperor's New Clothes*," I said. "You remember—everybody felt he had to pretend the Emperor was fully clothed to protect himself from being thought unfit for his job, and then the little boy said—"

"It wasn't a boy, it was a girl, Ma," Helen interrupted.

I sighed. *"It was a boy,"* I said. "Not that it makes any conceivable difference."

Helen treated me to the pitying look she had begun to effect which said plainer than words: Poor Ma—it must be awful to be getting so old and losing your faculties.

"May I be excused?" Mike asked. "Me, too?" from Ruthie. And they retreated upstairs. That left six of us at the table, the baby on her father's lap, three interested spectators, and Helen and I squaring off.

"Helen," I said firmly, "now why are you so sure it was a girl?"

"Why are *you* so sure it's a boy?"

"Well, it's always a boy in cases like this. After all, he's only there to prove a point, and it's just like using 'he' or 'you' when you mean 'one.' "

"She's!" Helen said. "Ma, after all, I've only heard or seen this hundreds of times and it's *always* a girl!"

"Hundreds of times?" I asked, outraged. "*Hundreds* of times?"

"Oh, God," Pete muttered.

"Well, dozens of times, anyway."

"Name one," I demanded.

"Well, Ma," Helen said in an injured tone, "I can't remember offhand like this. I just *know* it was a girl!"

"You know! That is very fishy proof. Nobody can pin it down. In fact, it's demagogical."

"What's demagogical?" Katy asked.

"Well, it's something like Hitler or McCarthy would use. Like rumoring, sliding out from having to show any facts—"

Helen stood up panting. "Oh," she wailed, "oh! Now you've gone too far, Mother, you really have. How can you say a thing like that to your own daughter. Telling me I'm like Hitler!"

Jean pulled at my arm. "Ma," she said, "look, Ma." I hadn't noticed she had left the table, but she had found her book, her old dog-eared H. C. Andersen, and she was offering it to me.

She laid it open in front of me, and a big bright smile stretched over her face.

Feeling completely foolish, I read the following passage: " 'But he has got nothing on,' " said a little child. " 'Oh listen

61

to the innocent,' " said its father. And one person whispered to the other what the child had said. " 'He has nothing on—a child says he has nothing on!' "

Nobody could speak for a moment. Then we began to laugh.

All of a sudden Helen's eyes narrowed.

"Where's the *Danish* book? Jean, go get the Danish book!"

Jean ran for that.

"Et lille barn," H. C. Andersen had written, "a little child."

There was a long silence.

"Okay, do the dishes," I said after a while, "it's eight o'clock."

I sat down with the paper, but couldn't keep my mind on it because Helen kept poking her nose out of the kitchen and saying, "Ha!"

"Don't rise to it," Pete warned me. "Just let it all die down!"

But on about the fifth "Ha!" I rose.

"What does that 'Ha!' mean?" I asked crossly. "After all you were wrong, too!"

"Yes, but *you* weren't right, either." she said triumphantly.

I felt helpless under such maddening logic.

"I'm getting an awful headache," I said to Pete. "I think I'll take a couple of aspirin and turn in or else I'll just get up and start banging my head on the wall."

The next evening, Pete came home with a seventeen-inch television set which he installed immediately. We all hurried through the meal and the dishes in fine good humor and, at ten minutes to eight, there we were, ranged around it, drinking in the test pattern, jumping up to twiddle dials, just like every other fortunate family in good old Denmark.

# 5. DANISH IS EASY
# FOR THE DANES

DANES WILL TELL YOU THAT DANISH ISN'T A LANGUAGE; IT'S
a disease of the throat. I can't count the times I heard this
remark from well-educated Danes. Less well-educated Danes
confide with awe that, next to Chinese, Danish is the most
difficult language in the world. They seem quite proud of
their precocity in learning it.

For a person like me who was born on the South Shore

of Massachusetts and spent the first eighteen years of her life ignoring her throat and talking freely through her nose, there was a great deal of truth in the first observation. Where I grew up, if you didn't talk through your nose, you had an accent. Consequently, it was not until I arrived at Radcliffe that I was informed it was *I* who had the accent. Moreover, it was a thoroughly unpleasant one and I had to go to a speech class to get rid of it since Radcliffe didn't want her representatives to sound like clam diggers. There was only one other girl in the speech class and she came from *way* down on Cape Cod. I had to laugh at her accent when the instructor played back the record we had made of a little verse:

> "Ann, Ann, come quick as you can.
> There's a fish that talks in the frying pan.
> Out of the fat as clear as glass
> He raised up his head and said, 'Alas!' "

If my A's were flat, Miss Hinckley's were prostrate!

"Now, Miss Hinckley," said the instructor whose mouth was so full of hot potato he could hardly force out the words, "whose tone is the more nasal—yours or Miss Bodell's?"

"Miss Bodell's," said she, giving me a devilish look.

My mouth opened in an unbelieving O. What nerve she had!

"To tell you the truth," said the instructor, "I hear little difference. Now, each of you try it this way,

> "Awn, Awn, come quick as you cawn,
> There's a fish that tawks in the frying pawn.
> Out of the fawt as clear as glawss,
> He raised up his head and said, 'Alaws.' "

Awfter the clawss, we were both a little disconsolate.

"Let's go down to Daley's and get a cup of coffee," Miss Hinckley said, "my throat feels as tight as a clawm. If I end up talking like him, I'll never dare go back to Truro!"

To be sure I grew a little less nasal over the years, living as I did in different parts of the country. But my throat never got a real workout again until the year we lived in Denmark and I began to take Danish lessons from a neighbor.

"Everything must come from the throat," Fru Bundgaard told me, "especially the ø sound." (To approximate ø in English, say "er" while gargling.) "When you pronounce words like brød (bread), smør (butter), and børn (children), pretend that you are going to be sick to your stomach. That's exactly it!"

Another throat workout in Danish is the stød or glottal stop which seems to be thrown in here and there without any reason. If you say "California oranges" what happens to your throat between the two words is the glottal stop. Used conscientiously, it sounds like a bad case of hiccups or extreme exhaustion.

I tried valiantly for Fru Bundgaard and the more disgusting I sounded, the prouder she was of me. However, it was a bit difficult keeping my lunch down, and I was much too self-conscious when talking to anyone other than Fru Bundgaard to put the needed feeling into my Danish.

Aside from its pronunciation, Danish isn't a difficult language. Grammatically it is simpler than French or German. It has a small vocabulary. There being no word for baby, you call a baby a littlechild. Pink is lightred. This process of stringing words together to produce other words can be carried to great lengths. It kills you at first. You get some beauties on the shop signs: *Herrerekviperingshandler*, for example, which means gentleman's outfitter. After awhile, however, you become expert at breaking up these mouthfuls.

My husband and I were determined to learn Danish well enough to be able to read newspapers, conduct transactions in stores and have simple conversations with people on buses and streetcars. Thus the summer before we embarked for Europe, we went through a phonograph record course in Danish. Each evening Pete and I—and sometimes the children—sat before the machine listening and repeating. Mornings in California I went about my housework to the accompaniment of the records and eventually had all the easy ones by heart. So by the time we got to Denmark we thought we knew how to count, tell time, and make change with *kroner* and *øre*. We were sure we could ask in Copenhagen restaurants for beer, coffee, cucumber salad and roast lamb, and we tried to. *How* we tried! But no one would let us. As soon as we opened our mouths in Danish, we were answered in English or an English speaker was fetched in a hurry.

On the other hand, when I visited the shops in our little town of Hørsholm where none of the shopkeepers spoke English, I couldn't understand *their* Danish.

"*Goddag*," said the young lady in the bakery, smiling pleasantly, "*Ovaskadavare?*" I knew she was asking me what I wanted but, to save my life, I couldn't figure out the exact words she was saying. It didn't sound like anything the man on the phonograph record had said. I snapped out of my puzzlement and ordered. That was easy. You just pointed to what you wanted and said, "Dem der" ("them there.") And instead of attempting the numbers, which seemed to make the clerks uneasy, you held up a few fingers. When you received your goods, they wrote the price on a piece of paper; you paid, said *"Tak"* ("thank you") and they said *"Selv tak."* ("Don't mention it!")

But *ovaskadavare?* That was a corker. I muttered it to myself all the way home and at odd moments during the day. It popped into my mind when I was in bed and delayed sleep. And then a couple of days later, a light went on in my head and illuminated letters suddenly spelled out, "Og hvad skal det vaere?" I snapped my fingers triumphantly. Of course! "And what shall it be?" That was exactly what the man said on the record. Only it sounded different when a woman said it, and she had tacked on an "and" before the phrase! I laughed aloud and felt victorious. It was the breakthrough!

After that, and because Fru Svendsen's understanding of my Danish had boosted my morale, I got bolder in the shops. No longer did I simply point and mutter "Dem der!"

*"Jeg vil gerne have to agurker,"* I told the girl in the greengrocer's. And she actually got me two cucumbers, smiling broadly, as proud of me as I was. I attempted slight conversations.

*"Vejret er fint idag,"* ("It's a nice day") I ventured to the clerk at the Irma, a small self-service grocery.

*"Ja, det er det,"* she answered carefully. *"Kan De lide lille*

*Danmark?"* ("Do you like little Denmark?")

*"Ja!"* I answered fervently. *"Det er et dejligt land!"* ("Yes, it's a lovely country.")

Tiny successes spurred us on. Every night my husband brought home a newspaper, sometimes *Berlingske Tidende,* sometimes *Politiken,* and after dinner, I settled down with it and the dictionary. The paper contained a whole new vocabulary—words to do with the government and international affairs, sports, crime, and agriculture. It was hard going. I saved idiomatic expressions not explained by the dictionary to show Fru Svendsen. She expanded on them, explained the co-operatives and the current agricultural situation, always the most important news in Denmark.

Perfidious Albion began sending her old dairy cows to Southern Europe to be sold for meat. This had been Denmark's monopoly. If the price of butter and bacon went down in England, gloom reigned in Denmark. Danish blue cheese was selling in the United States for less than American-produced blue cheese. And in France, housewives ignored the cheaper Danish *Samsø* in favor of their more expensive domestic cheeses although Danish cheese was obviously superior.

What could be done about these problems? The answer, said one writer, was advertising. Evoking snob appeal. And also raising the prices. Denmark was behind the times. She was far too modest.

I immersed myself in Denmark's troubles, eagerly following her politics and the course of her agricultural headaches every evening, and in a short while I was able to get through a Danish newspaper in about the same length of time I could read an American one. My syntax improved, my vocabulary built up.

But still, every time I spoke to a clerk in Illum's or Magazin du Nord, Copenhagen's two largest department stores, I was answered in English or by the disappearing back of the clerk running to get an English speaker. It was discouraging, particularly since our children seemed to have no trouble at all in being understood. Their grammar was lousy. Every time they didn't know a Danish word, they just slipped in an English one. I'd go into the teen-age section at Illum's with Helen or Katy. I'd tell the clerk in Danish that we'd like to look at blouses, for instance. A lost expression would come over her face. Then Helen or Katy would repeat exactly what *I'd* said. The lost expression would be replaced with a smile and we would be shown the blouses.

Any time the children wanted to get a laugh from their friends, they would tell me to say "*rødgrød med fløde.*" This means "red fruit sauce with cream," and it contains nearly every difficult sound in the Danish language—the r rolled in the front of the mouth, and rippled over the tongue to the back of the throat where the ø is regurgitated, the d which isn't a d at all but a th checked almost before you've got around to saying it.

We were told that nobody but a born Dane could pronounce this phrase correctly, and that during the Occupation, it tripped up lots of spies. It evidently didn't trip up our children. But when Pete and I attempted it, the result was better than a circus. Danes and our children broke down completely. I'd been through that mill before—in our own country. People in the Middle West and in the West were always demanding that I say, "park your car on Park Street," "men of Harvard," or some such assemblage of hilarious sounds.

A month or so after our arrival in Europe, we went to have tea with the sister of my next-door Danish neighbor back in California. She proved to be an elegant lady in her fifties, wearing a pale green cashmere sweater, a string of matched pearls and soft Italian-made shoes. She lived with her husband and son in an apartment near Norreport station which was not impressive from the outside but inside looked like a cozy corner of an inhabited palace. We were served tea from an antique silver service.

I loved hearing her Danish, but she insisted on speaking English to us, although she had forgotten most of it and had to grope after every other word and drag it crackling through her throat. Listening to this painful process strengthened my confidence in my Danish, so I let them have a fluent burst of it.

There was a stunned silence. She stared at me, then groaned, "Oh no! My dearrr tchildt! I could nott—bearrr it!"

"Well," my husband consoled me as we tramped down the stairs an hour later, "you tried, anyhow. That's something. And they *are* awfully nice people. You enjoyed yourself, didn't you?"

"Sure," I said, "after I got my breath back. But what I

can't reason out is why certain people like Fru Svendsen, for instance, understand me with no trouble at all, and the storekeepers around Hørsholm—"

"Well, they *have* to understand you," he said. "They can't speak any English."

"What about the people in the stores in Copenhagen who don't speak English?"

"They can always get someone who does," he shrugged. "Why should they strain themselves?"

Pete made few attempts to speak Danish with his colleagues at the University. Their English was too good and they enjoyed practicing it. So he contented himself with acquiring a reading knowledge of Danish and the ability to order beer and *smørrebrød* in restaurants. On the way home from work on the train, he read the paper like any commuter. Each coach on the Danish trains was divided into *Rygere* (smoking) and *Ikke Rygere* (no smoking). There is no point in trying to pronounce these words. To begin with, the k's are pronounced like g's, and g's are pronounced like y's—I'll let it go at that.

For me, taking the train to Copenhagen was a fascinating experience and en route I wasted no time in reading. From the moment of arrival in the crisp morning at our local railroad station, through the adventure of buying the ticket and pronouncing *København*—never think you are approximating the Danish when pronouncing Copenhagen, Copen-*hah*gen through hearing the announcer bark "*Toget imod København!*" to scrambling for a seat in the *Rygere*, I was enthralled. The *Ikke Rygere* I avoided. It catered to children and genteel ladies and gave you no sense of high adventure.

But in the morning and late afternoon, the *Rygere* was full of businessmen, handsome, well dressed and extremely masculine. They immediately lit up small cigars, sufficient for the thirty-minute trip, and the car filled up with rich smoke and the rumble of throaty butter and egg talk. I'd strain to understand, but got only key words: *marked* (market), *skat* (tax), *penge* (money), and *kroner* (crowns). By the end of the trip I was half-asphyxiated and could barely see through the blue clouds and my head reeled with smoke and hints of high finance.

Naturally, all our family got proficient in money talk within a short time after our arrival. *"Naa, det er for dyrt!"* ("Oh, that's too expensive!"), *"Har De noget billiger?"* ("Have you something cheaper?"), *"Hvad koster den?"* ("What does it cost?") tripped off our tongues with no trouble at all and everybody understood these phrases.

One day, my husband and I were having a cup of coffee in the Copenhagen railroad café before taking our train back home. We eavesdropped on the conversation of four ladies at the next table. They were comparing bargains of the day's shopping, and *penge, kroner, dyr* and *billig* pelted us thick and fast. Then they began to divvy up their tea check and grew extremely confused as to who owed whom what, counting on their fingers and shoving little piles of *kroner* and *øre* back and forth across the table.

"Have you noticed how everywhere you go they're talking about nothing but money?" I asked my husband *sotto voce* in English.

As one, the four ladies stopped their figuring and looked at me startled. Then they burst into laughter. One shook her finger at me as they got to their feet.

"Oh, you are naughty!" she chided in English and they left, casting pleased glances at us over their shoulders. Pleased because they were so good at English. They had not taken the least offense at my observation.

As a matter of fact, I had been about to philosophize that most of the small talk of the whole human race is based on money and in the end everything, no matter how nobly begun, shakes down to finance. Scarcely an original thought. But it explained why the phrases concerning money came so readily to my ear and tongue. If you use a word or a phrase thirty times, it's yours for keeps, I've heard. And by the time we'd been in Denmark two months, we'd used the money phrases *thirty* times thirty times. Not so the exalted phrases unfortunately, except for the word *tak* (thanks) which means, also, please. Scandinavians can say thanks into infinity. "Thanks thanks," they say, "Thanks you shall have,' "A thousand thanks," "Many thanks," "My best thanks," "Thanks for the food," "Thanks for the last time you entertained me."

Along with Fru Svendsen and the shopkeepers in our town, there was a second group with whom I could speak Danish. This consisted of people who spoke several languages, none of them well and sometimes most of them in the same sentence. I read French fairly well, German less well, and speak them both badly. Thus, there was a great bond between me and these people—we were all in the tower together.

"Oh, see how *sveet den lille knabe* helps *hans schwester*," said Fru Magnussen to me the first day I took Mike and Ruthie to kindergarten. She was the principal, a sweet-faced lady in her late fifties. I had been very uneasy about enrolling such young children—Mike, as I have said, was six and Ruthie only four—in a kindergarten where none of the teachers spoke English. Both boy and girl were rather shy and I thought they'd be scared to death. And they *were* scared that first day. Mike helped Ruthie off with her jacket, and they held each other's hand, their lips trembling, their eyes full of tears.

"They're so scared!" I told Fru Magnussen, apprehensively.

"How?" she asked, "*Hvad behar?*" (pronounced "*Vubba?*")

"*De er for bange* (They are so scared)," I said.

"Ah," she breathed gratefully, "*Ich verstehe* (I understand). *Aber, vi* be so *gut to dem!* They *snakker* Danish *snart*—soon?" She bent down and crooned to them in a language any child understands. "*Den lille* Mike *und den lille* Ruthie . . . so sveet! Come *nu! Vi* see *andre Kinder*, no?"

"Telephone *til mig*," I said, getting into the spirit, "*wenn dey for bange er* (if they get too scared), I'll *kom*." Then I backed out as she led them, by the hand to the play yard where the little Danes were playing in a doll's house and on swings and slides. Ruthie threw one anguished look over her shoulder, and I fled.

That afternoon when I returned for them, Fru Magnussen reported in English, Danish, and German, that Ruthie had cried two or three times and Mike had comforted her. The two of them appeared now, walking carefully as sleep walkers, faces stiff.

"What did you do?" I asked them on the way home.

"Nothing," said Ruthie in a faraway voice.

"Oh, we did too," Mike corrected. "We *leg*. . ed. That means played."

"Oh," I said, "did you like it?"

"No!" Ruthie said in a positive tone.

"It was okay, I guess," Mike sighed.

Each morning that week I took them to kindergarten, left them with many misgivings and turned up again at four to escort them home. I wedged my way past the youngsters spilling out of the doors into the hall where Mike and Ruthie waited, jackets on, silent and blank-faced, holding hands. That Friday, however, they spilled out with the other children, and Mike chuckled all the way home.

"What's so funny?" I asked. He tried to explain, but burst out laughing. He looked at Ruthie and she started to giggle, too.

"Come on, tell me." I urged. "Stop laughing for a minute and tell me."

"It's that Anders," he said and broke down again.

"Anders is a silly boy," Ruthie said. "He's always making the *Frøkens* mad. That's what they call the teachers. The *Frøkens*."

"Can Anders come home with us tomorrow?" Mike asked. "School stops early on Saturday."

"It's fine with me," I said wonderingly. "Did you ask him?"

"Yeah, I asked him and he said he'd ask his mother."

"How did you ask him? In English?"

"Yeah, I asked him in English and he said he'd ask his mother in Danish!"

"And he understood *you* and you understood *him?*"

"Yeah! What's so great about that?"

I shook my head in wonderment and began to laugh.

On Saturday, Anders came home with them, had lunch with us, and they proudly showed him the house and yard. He was a head taller than Mike and had a roguish look in his blue eyes. Mike laughed uncontrollably at everything Anders did, and Anders thought of everything. He clattered up the back stairs in his wooden shoes, making a fearful noise, and clattered down again, Mike and Ruthie close on his heels. They grabbed handfuls of raw cabbage I was shredding and pretended they were horses eating hay. Then Anders cried, *"Skal vi ud?"* ("Shall we out?") and they tore outside, whooping and racing around the yard. Anders saw our Volkswagen in the garage, and asked my husband if he would drive him home in the *bil.*

"Gladly!" said my husband in English. "Would you like to go for a little ride first?"

"Yahoo!" yelled Anders in perfect western style, and they dashed out and into the car.

"I'll be damned!" said my husband. "He understood what

I said! What is he—a genius or something?"

"He's a little pest! That's what he is!" Helen stormed into the kitchen, wearing her Egyptian costume, a slip made out of an old sheet with bands of crayoned hieroglyphics at hem and neck, and displayed a rip under the armhole. "Sorte and I were just getting ready for a meeting of the Sacred Order of the Pyramids and found those kids had got into the sacred boxes and ripped my robe. You can't keep anything in this house!"

Helen was coming to the end of her Egyptian phase the beginning of that year in Denmark. She was Suyakin and Jean was Sorte, and they always managed to be holding a meeting when there was some housework to be done.

"I can't get excited about a rip in your silly robe," I told her. "I'm glad Mike's found somebody to play with! And Sorte can't attend any meetings now. She has to go to the bakery on her bicycle and buy some bread."

Jean was the official bread buyer. She loved to go to the bakery because they always gave her kringles or cookies. She would come home with the largest loaf of bread she could find, balanced across her cycle like a chimney sweep's broom. She passed the time of day at the bakery and she brought home the latest news. That day she reported Herr Knudsen, the baker, had been cutting up some yeast dough and sliced right through his finger.

"There was blood all over everything, too!" she marveled.

"Oh, dear!" I exclaimed. "Did you see it?"

"No," she said, "it happened yesterday. His wife told

me. And he went across to the doctor and got a whole lot of stitches in it."

"And Fru Knudsen told you all that?"

"Yes! Don't you believe me?"

"Say 'blood' in Danish." I ordered.

"*Blod.*"

"Well, that's too easy. Say 'dough.' "

"*Dejg!*" she answered triumphantly. "Want me to say 'doctor'?"

"Never mind," I said disconsolately. "I wish I knew how you did it."

"What?"

"Talked with them so easily."

"Well, I don't know, Ma. Most of the time I don't know *what* the words are until they say them!'"


It was sometime in early November that I asked the milk boy to bring me a liter of buttermilk. I translated buttermilk directly into Danish, *smørmaelk*, and he didn't understand, since as I later learned *kaernemaelk*—churned milk—is the word I needed.

"Wait a little," I told him and ran to find the word book. Naturally I couldn't find it so I went back to the kitchen, took a deep breath and launched into an explanation of how butter is separated from cream, leaving, therefore, the product I wanted him to bring me. He listened carefully. Understanding dawned in his eyes even before I had finished, and he nodded with enthusiasm. He hurried out to the truck, and returned with a bottle which he handed me. "You are learning Danish fast!" he said respectfully.

I stood there exalted, flushed with accomplishment—until I read the cap and realized that what I was cradling in my arms was not buttermilk but a full liter of whipping cream!

On that gloomy November morning, I finally sat down and faced the fact that I was getting nowhere. Fru Svendsen understood me and so did a few select shopkeepers in Hørsholm when I limited myself to asking for cucumbers and kale and commenting on the weather. But that was it. And within me bubbled up ever vaster quantities of information gathered from the papers and magazines which I wanted to discuss with the man in the street, all beautifully phrased and grammatically correct. But there was no vocal outlet for them. Something was rotten in the state of Denmark, and it was turning out to be my Danish.

So, from blasted hope and discouragement, I began taking Danish lessons. Fru Svendsen seemed hurt that I was going to Fru Bundgaard.

"Why do you waste your money when I'm teaching you Danish for nothing?" she asked. "I understand everything you say perfectly."

"Fru Bundgaard says I don't pronounce things correctly," I told her. "Everything must come from the throat, she says. *Brød! Børn!*" I gargled. "Like that!"

"Naa!" she scoffed, "*Lad vaere med det pjat!* (Nonsense!) All those Copenhagen people, they talk so stiff. Who can understand them?"

"Can't *you?*" I asked incredulously.

"I can *now*, better than when I first came up from Lolland," she said. "Oh, that was funny! And when *I* talked, they could barely understand me. How they laughed. You'd think I was from Jutland."

"How do they talk in Jutland?"

"Oh, ridiculous. Some places in Jutland—it's an entirely different language."

This conversation gave me food for thought. Now that Fru Bundgaard was teaching me Copenhagen pronunciation, I had some basis for comparison. I listened carefully to Fru Svendsen. Since I didn't have to concentrate so hard on her meaning, I could hear the difference between her Danish and other people's. Hers was far prettier, I thought loyally; softer, more musical, without the staccato effect of the finest Copenhagen. She left the soft d off many of her words, so that *brød* became *brer* when she said it.

"Pete, do you think I talk like Fru Svendsen?" I asked.

"No," he said, "you talk just like yourself."

But the children pounced when I asked them the same question.

Helen snapped her fingers. "That's it! Ma, you sound just exactly like Fru Svendsen. I *wondered* what it was."

"Except for a little something extra that's pure Ma," Katy said.

They, of course, had picked up nothing much from Fru Svendsen. They were at school seven hours a day, and with their Danish friends a good deal besides. And, of course, they had been taking lessons from the school inspector.

Around Christmas time, we visited the home of one of my

husband's colleagues at the University. His wife, Gertrude, was a German girl. She had little English and had been speaking Danish for only a year. Her husband spoke impeccable German. He also spoke Oxford English, French, Swedish, Polish and Russian. Gertrude and I chattered happily in Danish the whole afternoon, while our husbands talked English and chemistry. We both found it delightful to talk with someone who wasn't critical.

Her husband's aunt, whom everybody called "Tante Lillemor," invited us both to tea one afternoon to further our acquaintance. She lived on a side street right off the main street in Hørsholm, and I walked over and found it easily. It wasn't until afterward that I found out she lived in the Old People's Home whose façade stretched along the main street. There was certainly no aura of Old People's Home about her apartment. She had two small cheerful rooms and a kitchenette. They were crowded with her family furniture, paintings and plants. Her tea service was the lace pattern of Royal Copenhagen and we ate *smørrebrød*, spread with a quarter inch of butter and topped with finely chopped kale and cress, pound cake and cookies.

Tante Lillemor had lived in France as a girl. Hence we spoke a comfortable melange of Danish, French, German and English. The general idea seemed to be, when in doubt about a word, reach in the bag and grab whatever comes first. The window was sometimes *vinduet* and sometimes *la fenêtre*. When we talked of buying shoes, we bought *sko* or *schuhe*.

I continued my lessons with Fru Bundgaard until February. We were going through Karen Blixen's *My African Farm*, a Danish classic. I would read a page aloud, paying scrupulous attention to diction, no matter how badly I strained my throat, and catching on to the rhythm and sweep of the language. Then I would translate. Toward the end of the lesson, we would have a conversation period, she correcting my pronunciation and helping me with idioms.

It must have done some good because soon after this I was able to do my shopping in Copenhagen entirely in Danish. My triumph came the day I bought a dress in Illum's and went through the trying on and the fitting to the accompaniment of much talk with the sales girl. She could not believe, she said, that I had been in Denmark only five months and could speak Danish so well! It was remarkable, especially since Danish was, next to Chinese, the hardest language in the world.

And on the street, in restaurants and stores, other words leaped past the money words in overheard conversations. Danes *were* interested in something other than money. They were interested in food, clothes, sex, television and bicycle racing. With a passable knowledge of Danish, you could talk to the woman at your cafeteria table or sharing your train seat, and learn every detail of her private life, including the cost of every stitch she was wearing. All she asked in return was the same information about you. A whole fascinating, intimate world opened up. In this world there were no secrets, there was nothing you could not joke about and make light of, even the King and Queen.

## DANISH IS EASY FOR THE DANES

You might be standing around noontime on the street in Copenhagen, watching a detachment of the King's Guard marching from Rosenborg Barracks to Amalienborg Palace —this is a small production compared with the splendor of Buckingham—not always in step and sometimes without a band. But there is a vibrancy about it, a gaiety and lack of solemnity that is peculiarly Danish. You'd like to get right in and march along with them! And among the people who pause to watch, you may hear some Dane remark, "A little sloppier today than usual."

This informality extends to the King himself. Frederik and Ingrid are the handsomest royal couple in Europe, but they don't act as if they knew it. We gathered with a multitude of happy flag-waving Danes in the courtyard of Amalienborg Palace to pay tribute to the King on his birthday. The Royal Guard was outfitted in beautiful crimson coats and performing fairly difficult maneuvers to the accompaniment of a splendid band. Quite sometime after his scheduled appearance and when the people were packed together like merry sardines, King Frederik appeared on his balcony accompanied by the Queen and the three princesses. He waved a napkin at the throngs and explained that they had interrupted him while he was eating his lunch. A giant laugh rippled through the crowd from front to back like a wave as people passed along what he'd said.

Of course, we were not in Denmark long enough for me to acquire much ease in speaking and understanding the language. Except for commonplace phrases which I could rattle off perfunctorily and which happily compose at least half of any conversation, I had to concentrate. Next to Fru Svendsen, I understood best the father of Katy's friend Birgit. He was a stout, good-looking, jolly man who had been a blower-up of railroads during the German occupation. His wife was blonde, plump and pretty, and made the best layer cake anyone ever tasted. The family collected American cowboy records, parts of which *we* translated for them.

After a few abortive attempts, I gave up trying to speak Danish with people who could speak English to any extent. Educated Danes—and by "educated" I mean all those who have gone through high school—are multi-lingual. In junior high school, they learn English and German, and they have lessons once a week in speaking Swedish. In high school, they get French. Other languages are not simply enjoyable frills for a Dane since, as Helen's English teacher asked, "Where in the world can you go and be sure of finding someone who speaks Danish?" Danes love to exercise their language skills.

All people have their tender areas of pride and sensibility. You can impugn the purity of a Dane's heart if you want to. He will admit he has doubts about his motives. You can impugn his morals. He'll get a big kick out of it. Insult him freely. He'll gleefully insult you right back. In fact, the better friends you are, the more outrageous the insults. The only subjects you must go easy on are nature, children and Christmas.

But question a man's ability to speak English, if he's an educated Dane, and you wound him to the quick. In attempting to speak Danish, you are doing just this, he'll feel, so you better have done with this nonsense and let an expert take over. You'll never be able to speak Danish the way he can speak English. And although I hate to admit it, he's right!

# 6. THE WAY OF A MAN
# WITH A MAID

JENS WAS FRU SVENDSEN'S OLDER SON. I WAS VERY FAVORABLY
impressed with him. He had curly blond hair and a pink
and white complexion. His whole appearance was fresh
and wholesome. True, he wore sideburns and a black leather
jacket, but that was no reason each time he came cycling
up our drive—he was the baker's delivery boy—for our
two older girls to run for cover.

89

"Can't you at least stay around long enough to say hello?"
I asked. "You're going to hurt Fru Svendsen's feelings.
What's so dreadful about him, anyway?"

"Ma, with those *sideburns!* Besides, it isn't only the way
he looks. It's the way he looks *at* you!"

"Oh, for heaven's sake," I said. "You're imagining things.
He's only a fifteen-year-old country boy."

"That's the worst kind," my husband said. "I used to be
a country boy myself!"

And then one winter morning, Fru Svendsen and I were
working together in the kitchen, she ironing and I peeling
apples for sauce. We got along splendidly in the kitchen.
We were never in each other's way, and we kept up a
comfortable chatter with friendly silences interspersing it.
That day I was telling her about the dark side of life in
America.

"In America," I said, "we are expected to spend half of
our time talking and worrying about teen-agers, how long
they should chat on the phone, when to begin wearing
high heels, what time they should come in at night. Now,
in Denmark it seems to me the parents just tell the children
what to do and they do it. They don't have to talk it over
with all the neighbors."

"Oh no," Fru Svendsen said. "My husband just says to
Jens, 'Now you come home at ten o'clock,' and Jens comes
home at ten o'clock. My husband won't argue with him."

"And teen-agers in Denmark don't have cars to get in
trouble with. They can't even get drivers' licenses until
they're eighteen. But in America—" I shook my head.

"Oh that must be hard. Think of all those teen-agers out in the cars. Tch-tch!"

"Children just grow up too fast in America," I said. "Now, in Denmark you see boys and girls of fourteen or fifteen, and they look like children still. They dress like children. They act like children. They're playing jump rope, not going around with lipstick on."

"I don't like to see lipstick on such young girls," she said in a shocked tone. "They *don't* wear lipstick in America when they are only fourteen?"

"Oh, yes, they do. Some earlier."

"No!"

"Yes, they do! And there's all the other stuff. Like— like going with boys so early, and—you know." I didn't know how to say sex in Danish. But Fru Svendsen understood. She nodded wisely.

"Yes. It's a worry. But you just have to tell them so they don't get into trouble. Now, when our Jens started to go around with Jytte, my husband sat right down and had a talk with him."

"He did? What did he say?"

"Why, he told him never to forget to wear a *gummi!*" she said in a surprised tone. Then she set down her iron and looked at me earnestly.

"Well, it just wouldn't be right for Jytte's parents to have to take care of another baby," she said. "All three of her sisters brought babies home. And the parents aren't so young any more. Besides, it's *expensive*." Her eyes flashed indignantly and she looked at me for comment.

But I was beyond comment. Her expression softened. "You understand me?" she asked kindly.

I nodded.

"It's hard," she said, picking up the iron.

"Yes, it is," I agreed weakly. "But didn't any of Jytte's sisters get married?" I asked, recovering.

She shrugged and grinned at me. "Later on," she said, "they all did. Don't worry about it, Fru Professor." In that moment she seemed several hundred years older than I.

"It was awful," I told my husband that evening. "You go along so placidly, shocking the natives, and then they let you have it right between the eyes. But I'm just a city girl. I read books—Proust, Freud, Miller, Kinsey—"

"You read too much," he said kindly. "Live a little!"

"Oh, keep still. But seriously, I'm *shocked!* Now every time I go past the school and see all those fresh wholesome kids playing jump rope and *hinklesten*, I'm going to be thinking these dark thoughts. You don't imagine Lise, Lone, Lene, Birgit and all the others—"

"Of course not," he said firmly, returning to his paper.

I picked up the home section and started to read "Tante Grete's Corner."

"Dear Tante Grete," wrote a *husmoder*, "I am having trouble keeping a girl. I have had five different girls in the last two years and they have all left for one reason or another—such as they are needed at home or they are going to the country. I do not think these are the real reasons. I try to be kind and not make them work too hard. I offer a very nicely furnished room near the bath. However, since the room of my two children is right next door, I do not allow the girl to entertain in her room. I do not think it right for a sixteen-year-old girl to entertain boys in a bed-room right next to the children's room. Can this be the reason they leave me?"

"That can *well* be the reason!" read "Tante Grete's" reply. "Her room is the girl's home! You should not only allow her to entertain her friends of either sex, but you should also offer coffee or cocoa and sandwiches!" I closed my eyes and read no more.

"How about the girls in your class?" I asked Helen in an offhand manner the next afternoon. "Do they go out with boys much?"

"Moth——er!" she exclaimed. "You see them all the time. Does it look like they go out?"

"Well, you can't always tell by looks," I said.

"Of course, there's Liss," Helen offered. "She went to her father's in Jutland for Christmas, and boy! what went on there."

"What? What?" I asked anxiously.

"We—ell, of course Liss is a year older and very so-phisticated—"

"Yes?"

"Well, she doesn't go for just boys. She likes older men. And it seems that all these friends of her father's were *very* interested in her."

"So what happened?"

"Well, nothing, if you mean did they kiss her or any-thing. They were just *very* interested—"

"Oh, for heaven's sake!"

"Well, Ma, you asked me, after all, and these men just swarmed around Liss—"

"Around *Liss?*" I said skeptically.

"—and she writes to this boy in France and the letters are to say the least—warm!"

"What do they write in—Danish or French?"

"Ma!—English, of course. And Ma, he ended the last one, 'I send you many kisses'!"

Time went on, and I didn't worry any more about Danish boys' intentions toward our beautiful daughters. There didn't seem to be any. Until Jørgen entered the picture. Helen just picked him up on the street. Actually, the truth was a little more complicated than that.

To begin with, it was spring. The sun was way up in the sky at last, strong and sure. There were delicate puffs of clouds around the horizon and the sky was clear pale blue. I opened up the windows to let in the fresh loamy smell and the birds sang all day. Wild swans flew over-head, making a sound like squawky windshield wipers. Living in California, we had forgotten how spring comes so suddenly back East. And in Scandinavia, after a dark winter, the people go out and sun themselves and walk forever, looking healthy and as proud as if they personally were responsible for springtime.

It was Easter vacation from school now and Helen and Katy had been invited to tea at Birgit's house. Helen's bike was being repaired, so they took the bus.

This story was told to us in a greatly detailed and con-

94

fused way, but essentially—

There were some boys on the bus and one of them was real cute. The boys began whispering about Helen and Katy who, of course, paid no attention to them. The boys got off where Helen and Katy got off and followed them all the way to Birgit's. They then waited outside during the tea. Helen, Katy and Birgit paid no overt attention but occasionally peeped out from behind the curtains, much to the disgust of Birgit's mother who had prepared a layer cake,* which, for once, they neglected.

After the tea, there were only two boys left waiting, the real cute one and a little shrimp. Birgit offered to accompany Helen and Katy to the bus stop, but the girls said they were not afraid. They waited at the bus stop, and the boys stood nearby laughing and kicking at stones. But the bus didn't come and it was getting cold and dark.

Meanwhile, at home it was dinner time.

"Do you suppose they're staying at Birgit's for dinner?" I asked Pete anxiously.

Naturally, he said he didn't know.

"Maybe we should phone," I said.

"Why don't you?" he asked.

We both hated to make a phone call. In the first place, we had too much pride to give the number in English and the operator never seemed to understand our Danish, so

---

* Danish layer cake does deserve a better fate. You take several thin layers of sponge cake and in between them, you put vanilla filling, preserves, chocolate frosting, almond macaroon crumbs and whipped cream. You frost the whole thing liberally with whipped cream, drift chopped hazelnuts over it and let it ripen for awhile in a cool place.

we always ended up getting the English-speaking operator and giving the number in English. One of my husband's proudest moments came the day he said over the phone, *"een og tyve, syv og tredive,"* and got put through immediately.

Anyway, I had just rounded up Jean to make the call—she had no trouble being understood—when the phone rang. It was Helen. She wanted her father to come and pick them up at the bus stop in Kokkedal. They had apparently missed the last bus. They were frozen, but the nicest boys had told them where they could phone from and would wait with them for awhile. And could she ask the boys to come over sometime?

"Yes, but not tonight," I said. "Now wait where you are and Daddy will be right there."

Helen's was the cute one, we heard later. Katy's was awful!

"What do you mean—mine?" Katy asked. "That little shrimp? I don't ever want to see him again!"

"Well, Jørgen's bashful and he won't come without Ib," Helen said aggrieved. (Ib is pronounced Eep.)

"Too bad," Katy answered, "that's not my worry."

"What did they look like?" I asked Pete anxiously.

"Oh, I don't know—just boys."

"Sure, sure," I said impatiently. "But—were they tall or what? Nice looking? Oh, you know why I'm asking! I just don't want those girls to get involved in something they can't take care of."

"Look," he said, "you worry about the damndest things!

96

They probably won't ever see those boys again."

The first time we saw them was just about a week afterward. My husband and I were coming home from the movies at the local theater. As we walked up the drive, we noticed that the lights were on in the living room. This was unheard of.

Two bicycles were propped against the wall of the house and, as we opened the back door, we could smell toast and cigarette smoke.

Helen hurried out from the living room, a delighted smile on her face. "Guess who's here?" she whispered, "Jørgen. And Ib." She made a face. "Come in and meet them."

"They smoke?" I whispered to my husband as we followed her.

Jørgen and Ib were draped comfortably over furniture none of us could be comfortable on, but they sprang up immediately and shook hands with us politely. I can't remember what Ib looked like, but Jørgen looked rather like a young Rock Hudson except that he was blond.

"Jørgen doesn't speak any English," Helen informed us, "but Ib does, *don't* you, *Ib?*"

We all stood grinning at each other for a while.

"Well, it's rather late, boys," I said weakly. Jørgen smiled vacantly. "*Klokken er mange*," I explained.

"*Ja*," Jørgen agreed. They made no move to go.

My husband was yawning.

"Don't make it too late," I said to Helen. We shook hands all around once more before we went upstairs. It seemed I lay there for hours, listening to the voices and laughter from downstairs, but Helen insisted that it was only about thirty minutes.

The next morning she told me all about Jørgen. He was fifteen. "Seven months older than I am," she said dreamily, "just like you and Daddy." He worked in a foundry, but she was going to try to get him to go back to school.

"I sure wish I could tell him to come over without Ib," she told Katy wistfully.

"Ib! Ugh!" they said jointly.

"Well, why don't you ask just him?" Katy inquired.

"Oh, great!" Helen said, in disgust. "Gee, you're bright, Katy. With Ib right there, I'm supposed to ask him?"

"I know, Helen. Next time tell them our phone number. Then when he calls, tell him to come alone sometime."

"I'll try," Helen said. "But I'll bet he doesn't even call unless Ib's right there beside him."

Apparently he didn't, either. The rest of that spring Jørgen was a frequent visitor to our house, but always with Ib. They would pedal up the drive about seven-thirty in the evening, just after Helen and Katy had finished the dishes. They always came into the dining room, shook hands and paid their respects to us and the little children, then they repaired to the reception hall, and Helen closed the French doors. Jørgen and Ib sat on the narrow French love seat, while Helen drew up one of the tea-drinking chairs. There would be the rumble of voices, loud hoots of laughter and then long periods of silence.

"What in the world can they be doing in there?" I'd

ask Pete after a silence. Then I'd walk casually across the room and steal a look through the French doors.

"They're just sitting there," I'd say, "sort of staring into space with little smiles on their faces. All three of them."

"Well, what did you expect to see," he asked once. "Them clutched in a mad embrace? All three of them?"

Along about eight-thirty Helen would make some tea or hot chocolate and take it into the reception hall, and at nine or so, Jørgen and Ib would come solemnly into the dining room, shake hands and thank us for a lovely evening.

"Jørgen isn't exactly a fast worker, is he?" my husband asked Helen along in April.

"Oh, it's that *Ib!*" Helen said. "If I could only get him away from Ib."

"Isn't Jørgen ever going to take you any place?" I asked her one night. "Two and three times a week they're *here*. It isn't that I mind. But I should think it would be so dull—"

"Well, thank you, Mother. Thank you very much!" she flashed.

But she worried about it too. Once she pleaded with Katy, "Why couldn't you just once take Ib for a walk— for my sake?"

"Oh no, not me!" Katy said. "Why don't you get Lone or Lise or Lene to come over sometime and take him off your hands?"

"They can't stand Ib, either," Helen said despairingly. "If only I could think of something. The time is going so fast."

It was. Seven months of our year was gone. In April we

99

went on our trip to Paris and London and when we returned, there were only three weeks left of our stay in Denmark. But Jørgen and Ib were still coming over again in the same leisurely fashion, as if there were all the time in the world.

Helen was growing desperate and her desperation infected me. It was getting difficult to be civil while shaking hands twice an evening with Jørgen and Ib, and it really upset me to see Helen peering wistfully out of the window at the white Scandinavian evening, with flowers perfuming it and nightingales making it unbearably poignant—and Jørgen and Ib cycling away down the drive.

"It's humiliating," Helen said, "it really is. You'd think I was a hag or something. What's the matter with me?"

"I can tell you," Katy said.

"There isn't anything the matter with *her*," I told Pete indignantly. "In my opinion, Jørgen's an oaf!"

"Will you just tell a mere man what it is that she—and you—want?" he asked. "I'm bewildered about all this."

"She just wants him to kiss her goodnight," I explained. "That's all. How can she remember a boy friend if he doesn't even kiss her goodnight?"

He shook his head, and began to laugh.

Helen drifted in. "If only I could get him to take me to the movies—*without* Ib! It's true he doesn't have much money. He turns it all over to his father. He just buys one pack of cigarettes a week and he cuts each one in half."

"Well, write him a note and ask him," Pete said. "Tell him *you'll* take *him* to the movies. I'll treat you."

"What?" Helen asked outraged. "He'll think I'm chasing him."

Then, just as we had decided we couldn't stand the strain any more, it happened. Jørgen called up one afternoon and invited Helen to go to Tivoli with him. Helen was beside herself with delight.

Tivoli is the most beautiful amusement park in the world. It consists of a few acres in downtown Copenhagen, bright with flowers and lights, and fireworks three times a week. There is a band concert, a puppet show, about thirty restaurants and outdoor cafés, and roller coaster rides cost only fifteen cents.

"I don't even care if Ib does come along," Helen said. "I'll push him off the roller coaster or shove him in the lake. And then," she rubbed her hands together, "I'll get Jørgen in the Tunnel of Love!"

But Jørgen showed up on Saturday night all alone. He was magnificent in his best suit. Nobody in the world can look as clean as a clean Scandinavian, and Jørgen was the cleanest Scandinavian I've ever seen. His hair and shoes glittered, his face shone. Pete and I watched them walk down the drive.

"Look at that!" I burst out indignantly.

"What now?" asked my husband.

Helen was wearing high heels and the drive was covered with gravel. There was one whole yard between Jørgen and the stumbling Helen and he was widening the distance rapidly.

"He could at least take her arm! I'll bet she can't even

*get* him into the Tunnel of Love!"

"You worry about the damndest things," my husband said.

They came home around twelve-thirty. At first we thought Helen was alone, because she began to talk the minute she came stomping through the door. "What a night! What a *wasted* night! Boy, did I ever pick a dead fish!"

She threw her purse on the table, shaking her head in disgust. At that moment, Jørgen appeared, all smiles, and came toward us, hand outstretched.

"Helen," I cried jumping up, "don't talk like that in *front* of him!"

"Oh, he can't understand," she said in a conversational tone. "He can't understand one little thing! Can you, Jørgen, sweetheart?"

He raised his eyebrows. "*Hvad behar?*" he asked politely.

"See?" Helen shrugged her shoulders. "Wait till he goes and I'll tell you the whole ghastly business!" We shook hands all around and Helen followed Jørgen to the door.

"Well!" She exhaled on a long sigh when she came back. She sank into a chair. "First of all, we got on the ferris wheel. You know how it is at Tivoli—two little seats, facing each other? Well, we get on where two sailors are sitting together. Right quick one sailor moves over and sits on the other seat. So what does Jørgen do? He seats me next to one sailor and he sits with the other, smiling real politely the whole time. So all during the ride, my sailor keeps crowding me. I have to keep removing his fat old arm that he keeps wrapping around my shoulders!"

"And what was Jørgen doing while all this was going

on?" I asked indignantly.

"Oh, he's finding landmarks all over Copenhagen. 'Look,' he keeps saying, 'there's Rosenborg Castle. Look! There's the Stock Exchange.' He even found the King's yacht in the harbor!"

"What else could he do up in a ferris wheel?" Pete asked reasonably.

"And then," Helen went on, shooting a mean look at her father, "you'll never guess! When the ride comes to an end, he wants to stay on for another."

"Oh, no!"

"Oh, yes! So here I am trying to fight my way past this sailor. 'No, thank you, Jørgen,' I say, 'I really don't care to.' 'Why not?' he says, 'Don't be afraid. I have plenty of money.' 'He has plenty of money!' the sailors keep saying, and everybody's laughing like it's a great big joke. It was just murder!"

"What did the sailors look like?" my husband asked.

"Great big old hairy things with beards. Ugh! Well, next we wander around. I don't think he's ever been to Tivoli before! He acted just like a tourist. So then we want to get something to eat and he takes me to Wivex, of all places. You know how expensive that is, and all he could afford was bread and cheese. So then I explained how when you take a girl on the ferris wheel, you don't let her sit with a sailor."

Jørgen was eager to go into the Tunnel of Love, Helen told us, but he didn't even put his arm around her. All he did was exclaim about how pretty it was. In fact, he insisted on going through again.

"So that's my big foreign romance," she ended wearily. "All these weeks and I never even got kissed."

Helen saw Jørgen a couple of times before we encamped for Norway, once again without Ib. I remember following their progress down the drive one of those evenings. Jean and Mike were at one window, Katy and I at another.

"Ma!" Katy shouted excitedly, "Look! He's putting his arm around her."

"No, he isn't," Jean answered. "She just fell against him a little. Look, they're stopping now. I think he's gonna kiss her!"

"No luck! She just had a pebble in her shoe."

"Oh, darn it! She's looking back. She sees us."


At last we closed the door of our mansion, never to return. After a trip to Norway and Sweden, we came back to Denmark and camped with our two green tents and Volkswagen at Nivaa Camp Ground twenty kilometers from Copenhagen. Here we saw Jørgen and Ib for the last time.

It had stormed and rained off and on all day. The rain would soak the tents and the wind and sun would then dry them. Wet or dry, we had to pack them up the next day and depart for Germany.

Jørgen and Ib had ridden out on their cycles to say good-by. We were all feeling blue; everyone had been coming out to bid us farewell. Fru Svendsen and her younger son Poul had pedaled away shortly before with many a precarious wave and backward glance.

It was now ten. In the pale watery night light, I watched Jørgen and Ib leave, hunched over their wheels. They stopped at the edge of the camp ground, waved, then disappeared. Helen stood for a moment, a tragic figure, and then rushed blindly back to the tents.

"Hey, Helen!" Katy called. "Did he get to kiss you good-by or did Ib stick around all the time?"

"Shut up!" Helen bellowed. "Shut up all of you, damn it!" and she dived head first into her tent.

"What'd I say—what'd I say wrong *now?*" Katy asked. "She sure is temperamental!"


Helen had a letter from Jørgen only the other day. He writes about once a month and sends a weather report.

My husband and I do on occasion read our teen-agers' mail. But we have talked the matter over with them and have come to a clear understanding. Anything that is hidden away between the mattress and the spring or in a drawer or pigeonhole, we do not trifle with. But letters left on floors, on chairs, on top of the range or the strings of the piano, we consider fair game. Thus are satisfied both honor and curiosity.

But back to the letter from Jørgen—it had dropped into the toaster. He says, in Danish, of course,—

"Dear little Helen— You can believe it has become cold here at home. It storms and rains. It was snow weather on

Tuesday, so you can think yourself how it is. I caught a cold, but do not lie in bed. I am still going to school. Soon have we Christmas vacation and that makes me glad. If only it snows and does not rain and blow for Christmas. Loving greetings and hail the family. Jørgen."

" 'Dear *little* Helen,' " I repeated to myself. "*That's* something new and encouraging!"

"Helen," I asked casually when she came home from school, "I'm curious. Did or did not Jørgen ever get around to kissing you?"

She just looked at me, smiled and went airily upstairs.

# 7. THE DARK POWERS

DURING THE WINTER MONTHS MY HUSBAND AND I HAD LOOKED forward to taking a two-weeks motor trip down into Germany when spring began. We planned it carefully and thought we had taken care of every eventuality, but you can't be sure of anything in this world, except that something will go wrong. Sure enough, as soon as we were out of bed that Wednesday morning in March, everything did.

The first thing we discovered was that the furnace wasn't working. When Pete went down to see why, he found the basement flooded. Being a strong-minded man, he waded right in to investigate the furnace and found, *mirabile dictu,* that it would work fine if he just stood there and kept pressing a button.

There was, of course, no hot water and since Fru Svendsen had stayed home the previous Monday to help on the farm, a big wash had piled up and Alice was out of diapers. Next, the American girl student we had hired to stay with the children phoned and said she'd had a stomach upset. She still intended to come, but after she had seen a doctor.

At this, I made my customary retreat to the Middle Ages. Our trip was hexed. The omens were bad. We couldn't possibly go away. The Ides of March had arrived. My husband and Fru Svendsen paid no attention to me. He got busy on the phone and she took off her shoes and stockings and began to splash around down in the basement loading the washing machine.

In a couple of hours, everything was under control. Men had arrived and were digging holes in the lawn to get at the sewer, the furnace was being repaired, and Alice's diapers were briskly boiling. Sue arrived, looking pale, but feeling much better. She had brought a friend who would stay the night.

There wasn't any reason for us not to go, and yet I felt reluctant. Fru Svendsen pushed me through the door and into the bus, briskly offered me Alice to kiss good-by and we were off.

I brooded all the way to Copenhagen. "I still think we shouldn't be doing this," I muttered.

"Now, why do you say that?" asked my husband. "What could we do that hasn't been done? Suppose we had left yesterday? They'd have had to manage by themselves, and we'd never know anything had gone wrong until we got back. It isn't as if any of the kids were sick."

"I know all that," I said impatiently. "I'm not worrying about that!"

"Then what *are* you worrying about?"

"Oh, skip it," I said, "if you don't know, I just can't explain." My husband is a rational man and will have no truck with the powers of darkness. "All I know is, I have to worry awhile and get it out of my system."

"Suit yourself," he shrugged.

We had lunch at Køge, shrimp *smørrebrød*, beer, pastries and coffee. It was risky on such an unlucky day, but I detected no signs of food poisoning. In fear and trembling, I called home to learn that everything was fine. In spite of our late start, we had made such good time on the road that we were able to visit the Holmegaard glass factory at Naestved, a fascinating place, but with danger lurking on every side. We were allowed to meander around by ourselves, taking no precautions whatsoever, while fourteen-year-old boys darted and dodged around us expertly, bearing long pipes tipped with blobs of molten glass. By ourselves, we explored the milk-bottle factory where the whole operation had been taken over by uncanny machines, creatures with snapping jaws and lunging pistons.

Pete got right up close to them and examined them thoroughly, but I did not trust them. They seemed so monstrously human, I thought they'd stop and ask for lunch and we'd be it!

By the time we'd left Naestved, I began to relax. At Vordingborg, we went up in the goose tower, the only remaining part of a medieval castle. Busy Christian IV had torn down all the rest, darn him. The castle had been built by Valdemar Atterdag in the late Middle Ages. He was an endearing fellow whose name "Other Day" was attached to him because of his habit of saying, "*I morgen er atter dag.*" ("Tomorrow is another day!") From the tower, topped by a golden goose, we had a beautiful view of the Storstromsbro, the longest bridge in Europe, which connects the islands of Zealand and Falster.

At sundown, we arrived at Gedser, the point where we would take the ferry across to Germany. The sun was an incredible color, pure crimson in a milk-white sky, and it dropped like a ball into the sea, shedding no sunset clouds.

There is one thing to do on the Gedser-Grossenbrode ferry, and that is eat. A vast smorgasbord is spread in the dining salon, and there are three hours in which to make the most of it. Happily we settled with loaded plates at a table which bore an American flag and which we shared with two American Air Force officers. The conversation, the delicious food and the beer combined to smother my last apprehensions. My worrying session had evidently been adequate in appeasing whatever dark spirits had needed appeasing.

The officers departed for their train below and we heaved ourselves to our feet.

"I beg your pardon," said a voice behind us, "I guess you folks are Americans!" We turned around to discover a very young GI with a wide-eyed, dewy, somewhat fuzzy aspect. He told us that he was returning from a holiday in Copenhagen and he had just discovered that the train he was on did not stop at Lubeck where he was stationed. He asked if we would give him a ride to Lubeck. We told him we'd be delighted.

By the time we were off the ramp and waiting at German customs, we had become his foster parents.

"Boy," he confided, "it sure is wonderful talking to you folks. Listening to that good old American accent. Makes me homesick for my folks. It sure seems like a long time." He was leaning forward and his head was almost tucking itself down on my shoulder. I couldn't even turn and look at him without bumping noses.

"Do you have much longer over here?" I asked the windshield.

"Only one more month, but, boy, it seems like a year." He hitched himself incredibly closer. I could feel his breath in my ear. "I sure can't wait to get back to the good old U.S.A. and get some of my mom's cooking!" I edged toward the door and looked cautiously back at him. His face shone beatifically in the light from the customs shed. His Adam's apple wobbled with sentiment.

Pete was busy now showing our papers to the customs officer. The boy had hitched over toward his door and was again breathing down my neck. "Boy! I keep thinking what I'm gonna do when I get back. It'll be like old times. There's this girl, see—and, well, these frawleens are okay, I guess, but they aren't American!" This remark was a terrible temptation, but I restrained myself. I just wasn't used to boys his age, I told myself. At the same time, I was becoming perturbed by the behavior of the customs official. Something was wrong. He frowned and ticked his pencil against his teeth. But with my left ear occupied by tender sentiments, I couldn't manage to hear what was going on.

"Just a minute," I apologized to the boy. "What's the matter, Pete?"

"Oh, I don't know—something about the *steuerkarte*," he sighed, getting out of the car. "He says I'll have to go into the office. I don't know what it's all about." If there is one thing that scares me more than bad omens, it is authority in uniform. And my husband's back as he walked away from me looked so defenseless compared to the broad green back of the customs officer. My heart started to pound.

"—as I was saying," the boy was going on, relaxing, now that he had me all to himself, against the seatback and swinging one leg over the other, "ma'am? As I was saying, these frawleens are okay, and some of them are sure stacked —pardon me ma'am, but you know what I mean! I mean, like they'll invite me home to meet the old man and the fraw. But I don't know—it isn't like home, you know?" He sighed profoundly. "You know what I mean?" He squirmed and scratched his head. His forehead wrinkled. "Like, well—just for an example, see, like when do they eat dinner?"

What are they doing to Pete in there? I was thinking. I could picture him standing there defenselessly behind a long desk backed with important green uniforms and Sam Browne belts while questions were shot at him like bullets. I stared out the window.

"—like when do they eat dinner, ma'am?"

"Oh, I'm sorry. I was just wondering what's going on in there. I don't quite understand what you mean about when do they eat dinner?"

"Well, they don't eat dinner. Germans don't eat dinner."

"They don't?"

"Nah! They got all this cold stuff. They got all this bread, cheese, radishes, cold cuts. You know. But nothing hot. See what I mean? Every time I go there for dinner—that's what they got."

"Well," I said doubtfully, "maybe that's just how it is in one family—"

"Nah," he said firmly, shaking his head. "I been to lots of families, up here and in Munich. And my buddies say the same thing. It's got me puzzled."

"What has?"

"Well, I mean, when do they eat dinner?"

"Maybe they eat dinner at noon."

"Nah! I thought about that. But they all work. They don't come home." He paused, considering profoundly, with wrinkled brow.

"I wonder what's keeping my husband," I said uneasily. The boy unwrinkled his brow and stared into space, his mouth open. All the other cars from the ferry had, by now, cleared customs. There was silence all around us. From the customs office, a laugh rang out. It chilled my blood.

The boy came out of his study and wriggled and cleared his throat. "Ma'am?" he said. He gave a little confidential laugh. "You mind if I ask you something?"

"No, go ahead."

"Well, I got this problem, see?" He wriggled again, irresistible as a puppy. "I kinda thought—like—well, you being a woman and all—you know what I mean?" I did not think this called for an answer.

"Well, it's this girl, see? Well, she isn't exactly a *girl*—"

My eyebrows rose. "Oh?"

"Well, she's a girl, but—well, she's the sister of this buddy of mine I used to have down there in Munich. I never met her in person, see? But, well, we've been corresponding ten months or so—and well, you know how it is. I've been writing *her* things and she's been writing *me* things—"

"That seems reasonable," I said.

"You get what I mean though!" He creased his brow. "Well, my problem is—do I owe her anything? You know? Gee, I wrote her a lot of stuff, but—you get lonely over here, you know? They ask you out to dinner and it's only cold cuts and you sit around after and look at the *fernsehen*—that's what they call the TV—with the old

man and the fraw right there all the time. That's *my* luck,
anyhow— You know what I mean?"

I didn't answer. The customs official was coming out of
the office. He was laughing and fairly dancing toward us.

"Ohh, your hussband isss zo ankry!" he told me de-
lightedly with a giggle. "He iss standink there and he iss
sayink zuch thinks! Oh ho ho!"

"But what's the matter?" I pleaded. "What's wrong?"

"It iss your *steuerkarte*, yess? You must pay much money.
You haff not paid for six months. Yess? Oh, he will tell
you. He comess zoon now!" He nodded and retired to
the side of the office, shaking with glee and stood there
with his arms clasped behind him.

"Boy! They get you coming and going all right," said
the GI hastily. "Well, as I was telling you—"

I knew it, I thought. We shouldn't have come! How much
money is "much money"? Oh, dear, dear, dear! Why did
we come when it started all wrong this morning?

"—get to go home in a month. Ma'am?"

"I wasn't listening, I'm afraid," I said. "I'm worried—"

"Aw, it'll be all right," he said quickly. "Don't worry.
Boy, speaking of worries, I've sure got worries. Well, when
I get home, what'll I do about this chick? I mean—I don't
want to get tied down. But I don't want to hurt her feelings. Boy, what a mess!"

"Oh, it won't be so bad," I said distractedly. My husband
was coming out of the office. "Maybe she's thinking the
same way about you."

"Yeah?" the boy asked incredulously.

"*Gute Fahrt*," the customs officer waved at us. "*Gute Fahrt*."

"And a *gute Fahrt* to you!" Pete muttered opening the car door. "Well, that was a nasty jolt. Let's get away from here quick!"

"What was it all about?" I asked anxiously. "Will we have enough money to go on? That man said you had to pay a lot of money."

"Deutsches Marks eighty-nine fifty, to be exact. Twenty-two dollars! For road tax! What do you know about that? For six months road tax on their lousy roads and we haven't even been using them! Our car is registered in Germany. Therefore they say I owe them eighty-nine fifty for using their roads these past six months. I told them I hadn't used their roads for any more than two days in September and I paid them for September when I registered the car."

"Oh, well," I said, greatly relieved. "Twenty-two dollars isn't so bad. I had visions of a hundred at least. That man said you got awfully angry in there!"

"I sure did," he stated proudly. "I told them what I thought and I didn't mince any words. I told them their roads were lousy, too!"

"Oh, you didn't, Pete!"

"I sure did!"

"Would you care for a piece of chewing gum?" came a voice from the back seat and a hand waved two sticks of spearmint between us. I took one.

"No, thanks," said my husband. "Care for a Lucky Strike?"

"I don't use tobacco," came the reply, "but thanks anyways."

Conversation lapsed while we lighted up. I yawned. It had been a long difficult day. I was glad we had reserved a hotel room in Lubeck because it was getting late. I relaxed, but my husband didn't. He was sitting bolt upright, making sure he got the most out of every bump and hollow in what is probably one of the worst roads in Germany.

"If they aren't going to repair their roads, they could at least put springs in their cars," he muttered. I didn't answer. I could feel the boy squirming and panting behind us, wondering how he could insert his problems into the conversation.

"*Damn!*" muttered Pete, having managed to find a particularly nasty rut.

"I beg your pardon," the boy asked eagerly, "would you mind repeating that?"

"Gladly!" thundered my husband, "I said *damn!*"

"No, no, no, no." I threw in hastily, glancing back, "You'll have to excuse him. You see, he can't stand spending money!"

"I don't mind spending money if I get something for it!"

I sighed and yawned again.

"*My* father always says," the boy put in masterfully, "they get you coming and they get you going. Ha, ha. And that's the way it is with this girl I was telling you about, ma'am. I was telling your wife about this girl, sir. Well, see, I was down there in Munich like I said, before I came up here, and they have this store called Walleck's down there in Munich where you get all these peasant things. You know. Well, anyhow, I sent her this big hand-painted box they had—it had all these hand-painted peasant paintings on it—and I guess she thinks it's like a hope chest—"

"Oh, dear," I said, trying to keep from laughing.

"You were in Munich, and now you're in Lubeck?" asked my husband. "Let me get this straight. Lubeck's in the British zone."

"Yes, sir. I'm attached to this British outfit. Public relations," he announced proudly.

Well, that figures, I thought.

"I sure spent a lot of money on that family," the boy went on mournfully. "I sent her mother one of those Hummel figurines. You know? Boy, I sure spent a lot." He paused to let that fact sink in. "*She* sends me a picture of herself finally last month—"

"Who—the mother?" I asked.

"Nah, this girl. All I ever had before were these snapshots. You know? You can't tell much by these snapshots. I mean—she at least wasn't fat or anything. Well, anyhow, she sends me this studio portrait. I guess she figures she's finally got me all sewed up. And anyway you look at it, boy, what a dog!"

My husband's face was twitching and I had to straighten out my own before I turned around to the boy. I could see his face dimly, full of tragedy, staring out the window at the forest bumping by.

"See what I mean?" he turned earnestly to me. "It kind of spoils going home, you know? And like you said, maybe she's afraid of me, too. I been thinking about that, but boy, not with *that* face, she isn't!"

"Well," I said lamely, "I wish I could tell you what to do. But you didn't ask her to marry you or anything like that, at least. It'll all turn out for the best!"

We let him out a couple of kilometers outside Lubeck. He shook hands with both of us vigorously and thanked us profusely for the ride. He hated to leave us, it was so nice being with real Americans.

"Well, you'll be home in a month," I consoled him.

"Yeah," he said, looking pale and haunted in the sudden light of the car. "Boy, the good old U.S.A. Well, thanks a lot, folks."

I yawned again and slumped down in the seat as we bumped and jolted along for another kilometer. It was just on the outskirts of dark Lubeck that we had the flat tire. *Jerk* it went in the night, scaring me out of a snooze. And then flup, flup, flup. The car made the music and my husband found the words.

"Well, you finally did it," I said. "Now you can really get mad!" And he did. But I wasn't worrying any more. The day had come full circle, and lots of worse things could have happened than a loss of Deutsches Marks eighty-nine fifty and a flat tire. The powers of darkness had declined a lot since the Middle Ages.

# 8. "QUE SERA SERA"

IF YOU TRAVELED IN EUROPE DURING THE SUMMER OF 1957, you may have seen dozens of Volkswagen buses, laden with children, on the highways and byways. That is, it's *possible* you saw many, but *probable* you saw mainly ours as we batted hither and thither, to and fro, up and down, looking for camp sites.

For instance, one evening in southern Germany, we

drove slowly back and forth on the same road five times, trying to find an elusive campground. Each time, we passed a slow-moving, leaky manure cart, driven by an old man accompanied by a blonde child in steel-rimmed glasses; they were much more delighted and interested in our comings and goings than we were in theirs. At every turn around, we fervently hoped that they would, meanwhile, have disappeared down some side road, but no, there they'd appear in the distance, inexorably coming, noisomely going, while we prepared by holding our noses and groaning. When we finally found the narrow dirt road with its minute sign pointing to the camp, they were right behind us. We exchanged waves and cheers as we triumphantly left them, feeling that we had known each other intimately for what had seemed a long, long time.

We were as awesome in our way as they were in theirs. On top of our bus was an oversized rack which carried two four-man tents, five sleeping bags, two double air mattresses and two single, two featherbeds, three blankets and twelve suitcases. As the summer bore on, my husband's stomach disappeared and his muscles took on stunning proportions from loading and unloading this gear twice a day. On the deck of the bus, we kept our cooking equipment and staples, a folding table with four stools, a supply of clean clothes, diapers, bathing suits, soap powder, towels, bandages, crayons and coloring books—we were ready for almost anything.

We left the first of June for a sort of shakedown trip in Scandinavia. We planned to drive down Zealand, cross to

Funen by ferry, then over the bridge to the Jutland peninsula and up to Aarhus, across to Sweden by ferry, on into
Norway, back into Sweden, and ferry again to Helsingør,
Denmark. At this time, back in familiar territory, we could
rest and size up the situation. Was it possible to camp for
the rest of the summer with six children? If not, what
*would* we do? Our passage to New York had already been
planned for on the twenty-second of August, and my
husband's Aunt Ruth was meeting us in Copenhagen on
the twenty-eighth of June to accompany us wherever we
went. So, on that sunny morning when we said tearful good-
bys to Fru Svendsen who was at work getting our Danish
house ready for its next occupants, we had already answered the question we planned to ask three weeks later.
Yes, it *was* possible to camp all summer with six children.
It had to be. We'd burned our bridges behind us.

We would not see the lime trees in flower at Birkehave
nor the snapdragons bloom again. I would never walk along
Ringvej of a summer evening and pick a handful of violets
or listen to the nightingales in the dark trees. The town
looked dear and familiar as we drove through. Neat housewives with ample shopping bags over their arms paused in
their rounds from cheese shop to butcher to greengrocer
to stare at us or to smile and wave. We said good-by to
the bakery ladies who gave the children a bag of candy,
and drew deep into our lungs the yeasty, buttery air.

On the way to Copenhagen, clouds gathered fast, and
by the time we reached the lab of the Teknisk Højskole,
there was an ominous feeling of thunder about to crash.

My husband had barely time to take a picture of his colleagues standing in front of the lab before the rain pelted down and the wind blew about with such fury that he fought to get the door of the car closed.

At this moment I remembered that I had packed all our rain wear in the boxes we had shipped to California.

"Wow, it sure is raining hard," yelled Ruthie.

"Daddy, are we going to camp in the rain?" asked Mike.

"Sure," Pete yelled back. "Why not?" He turned to me. "You have the raincoats anywhere handy?"

"I can't quite remember where—" I mumbled.

"Oh well," he said, "we probably won't need them today, at any rate. It's coming down so fast now, it will probably let up by the time we get to the ferry."

"How are we going to get our tents set up in the rain?" Katy asked.

"We'll cross that bridge when we come to it," said Pete. "Why is everyone so worried over a little rain? What's the matter? You all made of sugar?"

"It looks more like chocolate," I ventured, noticing that Alice's mouth was coated with a shining brown mixture and reaching for a Kleenex.

"It can rain for forty days and forty nights!" Mike informed us.

"Oh, it cannot," Jean jeered.

"It can so," Mike yelled. "Wanna bet?"

"It *cannot!*" said Jean, "God said He'd never send another flood!"

"Quit talking about the rain," I said irritably. "Why don't

you sing or play a game?"

They started to sing their repertoire of Danish songs. By the time they'd settled on the one that makes everybody angry, the rain had begun to let up a little.

The one that makes everybody angry goes like this:

"Oh, *Jean*, will you travel
On life's happy way
With *Kurt* by your side?
Answer yes or no."

"Kurt?" Jean exploded. "Why do you always have to say I like Kurt? I can't stand him!" And she yelled at the top of her voice:

"No, I will not travel
On life's happy way
With *Kurt* by my side
For him I hate!"

"All right, Helen, you're so smart!" She went on:

"Oh, *Helen*, will *you* travel
On life's happy way
With *Ib* at your side—"

At the mention of Ib, everybody exploded with laughs and jeers, and even before the song was finished, Helen screamed,

"*Nej, jeg vil ikke ride
Paa livets glade vej
med Ib ved min side
For ham haedder jeg!*"

"Why don't you ever sing it with Jørgen?" she added. So they sang it with Jørgen, and they all simpered and hooted unbearably as Helen with a fatuous grin and blush, confessed that, yes, she would ride along with Jørgen because she loved him.

"My God," Pete said, "is this going to keep up for nearly three months? We can't stand it!"

"Sing something nice and quiet," I pleaded. "Sing the one about the sun being so red and the woods so dark, with the little cat wanting to come in."

"That always makes me cry," said Jean. "How about the oom pah pah one?"

They all jumped hard on that and then they sang *"Que Sera Sera"* in Danish. That song had been played all winter over the radio in Danish, Swedish and German, and it irritated me frightfully because, after hearing it once, I couldn't get rid of it for the rest of the day.

*"Que sera sera,"* they shrieked, *"det ting det skal bli' skal bli'."*

The baby was going to sleep in the middle of the familiar din that was her lullaby. Looking out wistfully at the rain that was now falling gently over the rolling green countryside, the candy-striped red and white signposts, the low, u-shaped farm buildings with windows full of flowers and the unbelievably clean roadside with not one old paper bag spilling garbage nor even a rusty beercan, I was swept by feelings of nostalgia, anticipation and fright. I remembered that evening in spring over a year ago when we knew for sure Pete had the Guggenheim, and we dared at last to contemplate the possibilities.

We were lying in bed with the windows open to a warm night and mockingbirds singing. I was feeling as pleasantly tired and expansive as if I'd just had a baby.

"—and in the summer," I said dreamily, "we can take a long trip—just drive all over—France, Italy, Holland, maybe even Spain!"

"Whoa!" said Pete. "Hold on a minute! Have you any idea how much it's going to cost to take a family this size all over Europe? Why, just in meals and hotel rooms alone—"

"We can camp!" I broke in.

"Camp?" he said. "I never knew anyone who camped in Europe."

"What difference does that make?" I asked. "Europeans camp. There are camps all over! I read about it somewhere."

"Seeing that we've never camped before, don't you think it might be a little strenuous?"

"Pooh!" I said, "if I can take care of them all here, I can do it anywhere!"

A year later we were buying the tents in Sweden, the children were getting their shots against typhus, typhoid, tetanus, yellow fever, black fever and a few other diseases the foresighted Danes include in their three all-purpose doses, and we were studying roadmaps of Europe and booklets on camping. And here we were—on our way. It was raining, and our raincoats and boots were on *their* way to sunny California.

The sky was growing lighter as we neared the ferry which would take us across to the island of Funen, but it was still raining.

My husband rolled back his window and yelled out, "Stop raining!"

"Try it in Danish, Daddy," Helen said. "Say, '*Hold op, regn!*'"

"*Hold op, regn*," he shouted out. Miraculously, the sun broke through, the few last stubborn drops pattered down and everybody cheered.

That first night we camped at Bogense on the island of Funen. We had spent the afternoon in Odense, paying tribute to H. C. Andersen, and playing peekaboo with an old white-haired lady who had a fine arrangement of mirrors outside her window so that she could not miss a thing that went on in the street, even happenings around the corner. Bogense's campground was near the sea. A cold mist blew in, so I decided on a good hearty dinner of pork chops, potatoes, carrots and onions. It took Pete and Katy an hour and a half to put up the tents, half an hour less than the first time they had set them up on the lawn of our house. My husband was quite heartened by this and by the fact that there was no one else in the campground that night to watch his ineptitude. The little children pumped up the air mattresses, and then everyone demanded dinner.

But dinner wasn't coming. I was having trouble with the primus stove. I banged away at it and stuck a needle in the openings, but I could not coax up any more than a weak blue flame. We tried our second cylinder of gas, thinking that the first might have leaked, but got no better results. It took half an hour to fry the chops to a light beige, but they were still raw inside.

"Phooey!" I said, "I'll make a sort of stew. If they don't fry, they'll steam." Putting the vegetables in the bottom of our large pot, I laid the chops on top. Over an hour later, we were eating underdone pork and crisp vegetables. It's a good thing that trichinosis was banished from Danish swine twenty years ago and that the children liked their vegetables raw. We washed the dishes in cold water and went to bed.

The four youngest children slept in the bus, two on the back seats and two on the deck, which we mattressed with a featherbed, using another featherbed as cover. I lay awake for a long time, listening to the waves roll up on the shore and the birds restless in the half-night. "Please don't let it rain," I kept thinking, "not for a while yet."

Then, as usual, I let my mind roam over our family, picturing each asleep, the two little girls wound around each other on the deck, striped sandy hair mingling with chestnut brown, Jean curled neatly into a ball on the back seat, Mike lying blond and lordly on his back, Helen and Katy, each in her sleeping bag in the other tent. In this year they had grown taller than I and prettier than I had ever been. I yearned over them. Pete breathed evenly beside me.

"Let it be a good summer," I prayed. "Don't let anybody get sick. And *please don't let it rain.*" Then, realizing that this was quite a good deal to expect from God and nature,

I amended, "Don't let it rain—too much!"

We were in Jutland the next day, a high, sunny sparkling one. We saw the old fortifications at Ribe and storks nesting on favored roofs. If you want storks to live on your roof, you put up a framework on which rests a wagon wheel and if the male stork chooses it, he makes a huge spiney nest of sticks. Eventually the tile roof under the nest looks as if it had been whitewashed, from the droppings of the family. The storks like farming country where they can follow the plow and catch the mice and grasshoppers which have been turned up.

We camped at Esbjerg on the North Sea, and this time entered a community of tents, mostly yellow Danish tents. Ours were Swedish green. My husband learned, by watching a Danish family set up camp, that the floors of the tents must be pegged down first before the poles are set up front and back; and thus he and Katy cut their time to less than an hour. I was not so ambitious with dinner that night. We ate *wienergrød* from cans. This is a lamb stew with carrots and cabbage, and we had tomatoes and cucumber salad, with pastry for dessert.

While I was warming up the dinner, a lone hiker arrived. He wore khaki shorts and hiking shoes and on his back he carried a knapsack. From this he took a small silk pup tent, set it up in five minutes, dived into it with his knapsack and emerged wearing a starched white shirt, black shoes, and immaculate, freshly pressed gray slacks. He proceeded to light a small stove and brew a pot of tea.

"Hail Britannia!" said Pete, and he proved to be right.

The Englishman told us he was a journalist, hiking from Norway to Le Havre, writing a series of articles for his newspaper on the joys of hiking and making foreign friends. After that we half expected him to haul a typewriter and desk out of his knapsack. Instead, he brought out his dinner—a loaf of bread, some butter and Norwegian goat cheese.

We all went to bed soon after eating. As I lay in my sleeping bag, my mind was as serene as the summer night. It was going to work out just fine, I thought. One by one, all our anticipated difficulties were dissolving. We had begun to develop a routine. I went over it in my mind.

When we got up in the morning, we let the air out of our mattresses, dressed ourselves and then woke and dressed the children. Pete went out for bread and milk while Helen, Katy and I herded the little ones to the wash place and the toilets.

We breakfasted on packaged cereal, bread, butter and real coffee. We had our Danish dripolator, a cloth bag suspended from a frame. Into this I put finely ground coffee and got, even with *somewhat* boiling water, a strong delicious brew.

Then while Helen and I packed the suitcases, Pete and Katy struck and packed the tents and sleeping equipment, and in an hour after breakfast, we were shipshape and on our way.

Lunch we ate by the roadside. We set up our table and sat down on sun-warmed grass to eat, with enormous appetite, bread, cheese, sausage and fruit. In the evening, we could stop where we pleased, because there were camp-grounds everywhere. There was always a place for the eight of us to spend the night, and this might not be true if we had to depend on hotels. All in all, I felt quite self-satisfied, as I lay there in my sack.

Everyone was quiet in the camp and I could hear the silver sound of trees quivering in the slight wind. "It is a beauteous evening, calm and free," I thought of Words-worth's lines just before I went to sleep. "The holy time is quiet as a nun."

Suddenly I was awakened by loud roarings and lights flashing through our tents. My husband stirred beside me. "What's up?" he said.

We lay for a moment listening. Hearty voices surrounded us with song and laughter; enormous vehicles, Juggernauts undoubtedly, panted and growled, eager to trample us down. We sat up trembling. The vehicles stopped. But loud and clear came a voice not five feet away from us,

*"Nicht da! Heinrich! Hier haben wir einen platz ge-funden!"* ("Not there, Heinrich! We've found a place here!")

"My God!" said my husband, "they're invading again!" We peered out of the tent groggily. Two buses full of German youth had arrived and were busy setting up all around us a score of one-man and two-man tents.

"What time is it anyhow?" Pete asked, consulting his watch. "Twelve? Oh Lord. It's okay!" he yelled to muffled questionings from Helen's and Katy's tent. "New arrivals from Tyskland. Go to sleep."

We settled ourselves back into our sleeping bags. I turned onto my stomach and then onto my side. I began to itch. I scratched here and there. Pete was rustling and churning around too.

"I need a bath," I said disgustedly. "I'm breaking out in dry rot."

"*Que sera sera! All's was viert sein viert sein*," sang a voice practically in my ear as an accompaniment to tent stakes being pounded in.

"Oh no!" I groaned. "Now I'll be humming that damn song all night!"

"Be still!" bellowed my husband in German, rearing up on one elbow, "People want to sleep here."

"*Bitte*," I whispered. "Say '*Bitte*.'"

"*Bitte!*" he yelled.

There was immediate silence in the immediate vicinity. Then there were great hissings of "shh, shh" and much giggling.

We rolled around restlessly until all the goodnights were said. But I still itched. I poked my husband who was almost asleep.

"How *are* we going to take baths?" I asked.

"Oh, we'll hit a place with showers sooner or later," he mumbled. "Go to sleep."

"I wonder if they have showers in Aarhus," I said.

"Take a bath in the bucket tomorrow," he said. "Now, please go to sleep. *Bitte* go to sleep! It must be two o'clock."

I lay squirming while he began to snore gently. After I had given him the nudge that means "Turn over on your

133

side," he obediently turned without waking. I listened to his even peaceful breathing, and even that annoyed me.

It isn't only baths we need, I thought. We need clean clothes. We're going to have to stay some place long enough to get wash dried or else— Maybe we can find a laundromat. After all, they had them in Copenhagen and Aarhus is the second biggest city in Denmark. I'll bet we can find one there, too. Maybe even with dryers. Aarhus. I turned on my side which is the position I finally go to sleep in. Aarhus, I thought, hold everything until Aarhus!

I finally got to sleep, but we were awakened at six by loud calisthenics.

"*Ein! zwei! drei! vier! ein! zwei! drei! vier! Und zusammen! ein! zwei! drei! vier!*"

We crawled groggily out of our sleeping bags and got dressed. The sun shone down on oceans of ample buttocks in earnest motion under wash dresses and yards of sturdy legs under the highest rolled-up shorts. They finished their calisthenics, and then they had a wholesome, hearty breakfast—liter after liter of milk right out of the bottles which they waved like steins between swigs. They tore at *brötchen* with big white teeth while striding robustly about. I have never been so offended by simple good health.

They were as friendly as they were healthy, though. They immediately cleared their breakfasts from our table and benches and they gave us some of their milk. The boys crowded around Helen and Katy calling them *Fräulein* and asking them about their studies in America.

"*Wo wohnen Sie in Amerika?*" I heard one handsome

blond boy ask Katy.

"He means, Miss, where is your home in America," another explained.

"*Ich verstehe*," Katy said carefully. "*Ich wohne in*—Hollywood."

"Hollywood!" they echoed in awed voices.

I choked on my coffee.

"Why did you tell that boy you live in Hollywood?" I asked her later.

"Well," she said, "suppose I said Los Angeles. Do you think he'd know where *that* is? But everybody knows Hollywood."

After we washed our breakfast dishes, Pete and I took the youngest children and went up to Ringkøbing to see the sand dunes. Helen and Katy said they wanted to stay behind to rest and wash their hair. We left them sitting in the sun, surrounded by handsome German youth. We didn't see the Englishman at all that morning. He had packed up his tent and his tea kettle and stolen away before we woke up.

That night we all took baths in a bucket, standing just inside the tent door. I went through the suitcases and sorted out the dirty clothes, stuffing them into a canvas bag that usually held an air mattress.

"There just *has* to be a laundromat in Aarhus," I told Pete. "I can't possibly wash all these clothes by hand in cold water."

Aarhus has a university and a thirteenth-century cathedral. It is a quaint and charming town with narrow streets.

"*Aar*" means "year" in Danish, and "*hus*" means "house," therefore, presumably, Aarhus means "Yearhouse," but I don't know why. The truth is, I don't know much about Aarhus, despite the fact that we were there for three long days and three long nights.

Aarhus is a low-lying town on a bay. It was lush and very green when we arrived and we soon knew why. The campground was a few kilometers south of the city and consisted of two levels. The upper level, right off the highway, was small and completely filled with tents. We presented our camping papers at the well-stocked kiosk and were told there was plenty of room on the lower level and that it was much prettier down there. We drove down a steep curving road and were entranced by the scene below us.

There was a grassy meadow some fifty feet above the sea, ringed by the bluffs and trees. Tents of all colors huddled together at one end of it. On either side of the road there were level places sheltered by trees, each quite big enough for two tents and a Volkswagen, and from them you could see the white sand and craggy stone arms reaching out into the water.

"Don't let's camp down there," Helen said. "Daddy, why can't we set up here in one of those places?"

Immediately, as my husband hesitated, I saw the catch.

"Oh, no!" I exploded. "Who's going to haul a full pail of water all the way up here?"

"I will," promised Helen.

"Not me!" said Katy.

"You'll maybe do it once, Helen," I said, "and then it'll be my turn, and I'm darned if *I* will."

We pulled off the road and all got out. The children ran immediately to the building that housed the toilets, while the rest of us looked around for a suitable site. Helen and Katy chose a beautiful place under a bluff, but I was all for setting up right near the road as close to the facilities as possible, figuring that while I could take a walk for beauty's sake, I would rather not trek an urgent child over a mile of lovely terrain.

"Gee, Ma," Helen said disgustedly, "why don't we just spend the summer sitting next to the toilet?"

"Oh, come on, honey," said Pete, "let the kids have their way for once. It's nice and uncrowded back there."

"Okay," I said, "I'll leave it to you. You just set up anywhere you want *down here*, but not *up there*."

So the tents were set up about sixty feet from the road, cosily nestled under the bluff. I had to admit they looked beautiful, their fir-green color blending into the trees and bushes that clung so precariously to the steep hill behind.

"You sort of feel more secure with the nice tall hill backing you up," Katy told me. "And there isn't anybody around us, either."

"No snores in the night," said Helen, "and nobody tripping over a tent stake. Take a picture, Daddy."

So he did, and I must say that it is a lovely picture. There are the tents, side by side, oversails stretched tautly, small flags of all the countries we hoped to visit, flying from each pole. Another oversail provides a little shelter between the tents and tarpaulins are laid down for a floor to prevent dirt from being trekked inside the tents. We set up our table and stools under the shelter and piled the suitcases toward the back where they would be protected from the dew.

We do *not* have a picture of the tents two days later. It is just as well. For no sooner had I unloaded the cooking equipment from the Volkswagen deck than lightning flashed and thunder growled and fat raindrops began to whip down.

"We're sure lucky we got set up before the rain started," said my husband. "Looks like it's going to be a corker. What did you do with the raincoats, dear? We're going to have to go up to the kiosk and get something for supper."

"I sent them to California," I said.

"You *what?*"

"I sent them to California," I said fiercely. "Want to make something out of it?"

"No," he said, wearily shaking his head, "let it lie. Only tell me one thing. Why did you send them to California?"

"Well, it never rains in California in the summertime! You know that!"

"But we're in Denmark," he said gently.

"I *think* that's why I did it," I said. "I don't remember any more. Everything was in such a big mess. Clothes and boxes lying all around, and you kept warning me, 'Keep it light. Don't pack anything for the trip unless we need it.' And I just remember standing there and thinking it doesn't rain in the summertime and putting the rain things in the boxes."

"All right," he said, shrugging, "now I know!" He turned to where the children were prancing around in the rain, holding their faces up to it and squealing at every flash.

"Get in here, you fool kids!" he yelled. "Do you want to catch your death of cold?"

We herded the children into the tents where they began to jump up and down on the air mattresses with their muddy feet. Then we ran to the bus and drove up the hill, not speaking.

That night I heated canned soup on the table we had pushed as far under the shelter as possible and handed the soup plates back to the children in the tents. After that, we passed around carrot and cucumber sticks, and after them the cocoa. The soup and cocoa got spilled, naturally, not once but many times.

"See how steady my hand is when I take this cocoa," Mike said to his admiring younger sister. "See, I can even stand up on the air mattress holding it."

"No, no, Mike," I cried in vain. "Sit down!"

"Oops," he said.

"Oops," echoed Ruthie, tears of laughter streaming down her face, the hand holding her cup of cocoa shaking brown showers all over my sleeping bag.

"While you're getting the cloth, Ma," called Katy from the other tent, "I spilled a little noodle soup on the overnight case."

We finally got them to bed, unwashed but damp and happily hysterical; and when finally they were asleep, after many bedtime stories and ominous threats, Pete and I plodded through the mud and the steady downpour to the facilities.

"Lordy, lordy!" he said a few minutes later, as he settled into his sleeping bag, "What next?"

I wiggled my cold feet down into my bag. I touched something even colder and wetter and jumped out with a great yell.

"There's a snake in my sleeping bag," I cried with great shudders.

Pete struggled out, sprang to his feet, grabbed my sleeping bag, unzipped the tent flap and tripped over the raised canvas doorway. I fumbled for the flashlight and held it on him tremblingly as he got to his feet wet, muddy and swearing and shook the bag. Out slithered a large piece of peeled cucumber.

"There's a snake in my sleeping bag!" he said in falsetto as we lay at last, side by side. "Oh Lordy! I sent them to California because it never rains in Los Angeles in the summer! Ai yi yi!"

I maintained a hurt but dignified silence. I was waiting. Maybe he'd say it and maybe he wouldn't. But I was waiting.

"Snakes in the sleeping bag," he went on. "I sent them to California!" he paused. I waited. On and on he maundered about snakes and raincoats. And then, "Why don't we camp? she says. Aren't you afraid camping with six children is going to be a little too much for you? I ask.

Oh no, says she. If I can manage them here, I can manage them anywhere!"

I sat straight up in my sleeping bag. "That does it!" I cried. "Of all the *mean, lowdown* things to bring up. Now, of all times! And you're the one who's always saying to me, 'Don't bring up the past. Why can't women just let things lie?' That's a low blow, Peter, it really is!" I was crying and wiping the tears away on the sleeping bag.

He groaned. "Me and my big mouth," he said. "Oh God, I suppose we'll be up all night now. Come here."

"No," I said stubbornly. "Now I know what you think of me. I'm just a failure as a wife and mother. Maybe you should have married that Gwendolyn what's her name with all those itty-bitty blonde curls and those big flat capable feet!"

"Not that again," he groaned.

"Maybe she'd have given you six children and had the courage to take them all on a camping trip. Like fun she would. She's the kind who's always fussing around emptying out ashtrays and won't let you take a bath because she's just cleaned the bathroom. Isn't she?" I demanded. "Isn't she?"

"How would I know?" he sighed. "Eighteen years ago she invited me to a dance at Simmons and I haven't seen her since. Who's bringing up things now?"

"Well, you started it," I sniffed.

"And I'm finishing it," he said. "Stop it! Now we're both tired and our nerves are frayed. You've had your cry and now let's put Gwendolyn away for the night and go to sleep. Come here!"

Ten minutes later he was sound asleep, but I still lay awake, listening to the rain and some more subtle sound, a sort of trickling that I couldn't figure out. It gurgled like a brook forming underneath the tent. I reached my warm hand out from my sleeping bag and felt the floor of the tent. It was wet and slid around as if we'd camped on top of a marsh. The side of me that was next to the ground felt as if ether were dripping on it. Of course! The rain was pouring down that perfectly beautiful hillside we were camped against and running under the tent like a river. I poised a spiteful elbow ready to dig into my sleeping husband and thought better of it. He'd put up with enough for one night. I'd be a lady for a change.

It was still raining in the morning. We lay stiff and sore and listened to the sounds of revelry coming from the bus. We heard a door open and a voice loud and clear,

"Daddy, Mama, aren't you ever coming? We're starving."

We groaned and struggled out of our bags and into our damp clothes. I thrust clammy feet into sodden, low-heeled punched pigskin shoes, perfect for walking over Europe's cobblestones, cool in the warmest weather; fourteen ninety-five the summer before at Bullock's, Westwood.

Pete unzipped the tent flap and we gazed out at a sea of mud dimpled with raindrops on which tents appeared to float, and then looked up in horror at an enormous bulge in the oversail which formed the shelter between our tents. It now held untold gallons of water. Unthinking, I moved to shift the pole and let out the water.

"No!" yelled Pete grabbing my arm. "You'll flood the works! Better get a pan and dip it!" He sloshed out gingerly into the mud and looked around. "Damn!" he said. "I hate to tell you this, but it was a mistake camping against that hill. The water's pouring off it and running under the tents. That's why we're sitting on top of all this mud."

"Oh, honey," I said, "how awful!"

There was a clamor from the bus. "Aren't you ever coming?" yelled Jean. "We're starving!"

So, as I lit the stove and set on the water for coffee, Pete plodded back and forth to the bus, carrying bowls of corn flakes and milk.

"It can't last forever," he said as we sat later under the shelter, now lowered on one side to let the water roll off. Alice was sitting happily on his lap having cereal and milk from his bowl. I poured our coffee.

"I suppose we can't just go to a hotel?" I asked.

"What'll we do about the tents?" he asked. "We can't leave them and we can't take them down soaking wet. They'd weigh a ton. Besides, you know it'll probably rain off and on all summer and we'd better get used to it. That's one of the risks of camping!"

"As long as the children don't catch cold," I said, "and come down with pneumonia or something."

"They don't look sick to me," he said.

They were singing gaily in the bus, all bright-eyed and tousled, and jumping up and down on the seats.

Katy appeared in her tent door, rubbing her eyes. "What time is it?"

"Nine o'clock."

"What are we going to do today?"

"Well, after you and Helen get the breakfast dishes done," Pete told her, "we can all pile into the bus and get a good hot lunch and take a look at Aarhus."

"In the rain?" her voice rose. "Are you kidding? I'm going back to bed."

"Are you going to stay in bed all day?" I asked.

"Why not? I've always wanted to stay in bed all day sometime when I'm not sick. Hey, Helen," she called, turning back into her tent, "Guess what? Let's stay in bed all day. They're going in to Aarhus."

"What'll you do about food?" I called.

"Oh," her voice trailed out sleepily, "we can go up to the kiosk after awhile and get some *sodavand* (pop) and *pølser* (hot dogs)."

"Well, *I* am going to get all the dirty clothes together," I announced, "and first and foremost find a laundry. There must be a laundromat somewhere in this town."

I rinsed out the bowls and cups in rainwater. Pete put the baby in with Katy and Helen, who protested in vain, and piled all the suitcases into our tent. Then we collected the three younger children from the bus and plodded across the broad acres to the "facilities." Fortunately, it had stopped raining sometime in the midst of this activity, but the skies were still gray, obviously catching their breath to let us have it soon again. On the way back, we paused to talk to some friendly Danes who told us that we should never have camped so close to the bluff. "It makes the

**144**

water run down under your tents," they pointed out.

We thanked them for this information and, pleased to have been of help, they walked back to their own tent which had a wooden floor raised a good foot above the ground. Pete brought some straw and packed it into the biggest puddles and under the tarpaulin which served the shelter as floor.

The last thing I did before climbing into the bus was to trip on a tentstake and rip a two-inch gash in my pigskin shoes.

"What next?" I asked, rubbing my sore foot drearily as we sloshed and gurgled up the hill.

"It won't be so bad," Pete said. "We're getting all nice and warm and the rain has stopped. Pretty soon the sun will come out and everything will dry up. You can get the laundry done, we'll eat lunch, and then we can go to Old Town and see the old houses. Is your foot bleeding?"

"No," I said, "it's just a scratch."

"Are those all the shoes you have?"

"Well, I have those navy blue ones with the heels for more or less formal occasions."

"Ai yi!" he sighed and shook his head.

"Well, you told me to travel light!" I yelled. "So I threw away those old saddle shoes. I planned to buy some sandals in Italy."

"It'll be weeks before we get to Italy."

And so the first thing we did when we got to Aarhus was to go into a shoe store and buy me a pair of red *traesko*, the kind of wooden shoes that Scandinavian women wear while working in fish markets and beauty parlors. They had sturdy horsehide tops and thick wooden soles and heels to which pieces of rubber had been nailed. The salesgirl wanted to sell me some daintier *traesko*, heeless and with punched-out leather.

"But I want them for camping," I explained, "you know —tramping around in the wet dirt and hauling water."

"Camping?" she asked, "But you are an American!"


It is true that Americans do not usually camp in Europe. In our travels that summer we met only one American family, consisting of mother, father and little boy. They were Armed Forces personnel taking a vacation in Sweden. They slept in their car and ate in restaurants, so they did not experience the full joys or rigors of camping.

Later on in Switzerland, we saw a sign tacked to the door of the toilet which was printed in two languages. PLEASE SHUT THE DOOR, it said in German and French. Under this, people had scribbled the words in Swedish, Danish, Italian, Spanish, Polish, Czech, and languages I did not recognize. Gleefully we added the phrase in English.

By that time, of course, we were seasoned campers. We took cold showers whenever we were lucky enough to find a camp with them; we were able to set up in half an hour under any circumstances—on sand, on rock, on hillsides, squeezing into any available space, interlacing our tent ropes with others' tent ropes. And we washed our clothes with cold water in the same bucket we used to mix our salads in and hung them up on a clothes line stretched from tent to bus or tree or, sometimes, on the tent ropes.

But that day in Aarhus, we were as green as grass and I thought we simply *had* to have a laundry! We drove up one street and down the next until we finally found a place that looked as if it might be a laundromat. There was nowhere to park, so Pete said he'd hover just outside or drive around the block if he had to while I, with the heavy bag hoisted over my shoulder, went in. There were three machines churning wash but my heart sank as I saw they were professional machines.

"Do you have any machines that I can use myself?" I asked the woman behind the counter in Danish.

Her eyebrows shot up to her hairline. "Machines you can use yourself?" she said in a shocked tone. "No, we don't! I never heard of such a thing!"

"Oh," I stood in silence for a moment while her eyes ran over me up and down and sidewise: lank hair, wrinkled coat, gash in my shoe. "They have them in Copenhagen," I told her.

"Naa! In Copenhagen!" she said, her tone implying that anything was possible in Gomorrah.

"Well," I said, "how long will it take to get this bag of wash done?"

"One week."

"Oh? No sooner? Not possibly sooner?"

"Three days at the least," she said, pointing at the undone wash that was piled around the machines.

"We won't be here that long," I said. "Thank you." I hoisted the bag to my shoulder and turned to go. I hesitated. "And you don't know of *any* place in Aarhus that has automatic machines people can use themselves?"

She stared at me, shaking her head, and then looked hopelessly for someone busy in the back to protect her from me.

"Okay," I said, with a twitching smile, *"Mange tak,"* backing up, turning and running out.

My husband was coming around the corner. "Couldn't you just tell her what the story is?" he asked as we cruised around hunting another laundry that looked as if it might be a laundromat. "Maybe if you pleaded with her—"

*"Pleaded* with her . . . in Danish? You try! On second thought, no, don't," I said looking at his unshaven chin, cocoa-spattered pants and rumpled jacket. "If she sees you, she'll call the cops for sure!"

After three more tries in different laundries where practically the same scene was repeated—except for one place in which a man told me he'd actually heard of laundromats, but in America—we gave up and looked around for a workingman's restaurant in which to eat.

We found a pleasant place with clean flush toilets, a jukebox that had *"Que Sera"* in Danish, Frank Sinatra and Elvis Presley in English or a reasonable facsimile, and Ib Jensen, the Danish Elvis Presley singing my all-time favorite, *"Den Allesammen København* Rock and Roll."

This kept the children happy in spite of the fact that I

seized the opportunity to wash all their available parts in hot water. Pete and I began to feel human again after big plates of pork cutlets, pickled beets and fried potatoes. The waitress asked us about America, in particular, California.

"It doesn't rain at all in California in the summer," I told her.

While she exclaimed over this, Pete and I started to laugh, and she joined in. We laughed some more out in the street and in front of the store where a number of people were gathered around a window watching a television set. A camera was directed on the street just outside the store, and the scene there appeared on the television set. The children pranced and made faces at each other, seeing themselves appear at a different angle on the screen.

We bought bread, cheese, *pølser*, fruit and pastry, having decided against any more noodle soup and cucumbers for awhile. We looked at rainwear and then at the sky and didn't buy any. It would cost too much to outfit us all. We had got as wet as it was possible to get and it had rained as hard as it could already.

" 'Oh, it ain't gonna rain no more, no more,' " Pete began to sing on the way back to camp. We all joined in.

And then it started to rain again. "Oh, no," I wailed. The children groaned. "Damn!" said my husband.

We descended to the swamp. The tents came in sight, sodden and bedraggled. The flags dangled wetly, the shelter looked sadly rakish, with its corner tilted and containing a smaller but still impressive bulge of water. The canvas laid down for flooring was covered with drenched straw and gobbets of mud. Everything was a hopeless, incredible mess. I sagged, every bit of strength drained out of me. What a bunch of fools we are! I thought. Pete pulled up close to the tents, spattering mud, and stopped.

For some reason, I laid hold of the bag of wash as I descended. I plodded grimly to the shelter. From Helen's and Katy's tent came strains of song and laughter. Heaped outside was a litter of pop bottles and mustardy paper. I tightened up. My mouth set grimly. I pulled back the tent flap.

They had been reading magazines by flashlight. They looked up gravely. Their eyebrows rose. On each face had been pasted a tiny goatee and mustache cut out of paper and colored black.

Something snapped inside me. I loosened up and began to laugh—helplessly until the tears came. Pete and the children clustered around laughing, too. I let go the bag of wash; it fell against the tent pole that propped up the shelter, dislodged it and about three gallons of water slammed down, splattering everything in sight.

"Running water in the tents!" Mike yelled, and we all howled as if it was the funniest thing that had ever happened.

The younger children took off their shoes and ran around in the mud, squishing it up between their toes. We ate our *pølser* and bread without benefit of plates; the children played a game, dashing out into the rain, one by one, shaking a fist at the sky and shouting, "Stop raining!" in both Danish and English. I ran out and said it in French and Pete said it in German. Then the children performed an Indian dance, a "Stop Raining" dance, shouting and whooping in glee.

We then all trooped gaily to the conveniences, passing the trim, closed-up Danish tents.

"Look at those sissies with *floors* in their tents," Helen jeered.

"Now, Anders Andersen!" Katy said in a high artificial voice, "don't you go getting mud all over my nice clean wooden floor. *Pas Paa!* (Be careful)." And we all laughed some more.

Before putting the children to bed in the bus, we rubbed them down with a dry towel and gave them hot cocoa. Then Pete and I went to sleep immediately, warm and flushed with action.

Sometime during the night the rain stopped. A gentle wind sighed around the tents. I woke, conscious that something had changed, and nudged my husband. We unzipped the tent flap and looked out at the stars gleaming purely and brightly.

"Keep your fingers crossed," Pete said, "but I think we made it!"

# 9. IN HALF A LOAF
# OF RYE BREAD

THE DAY WE LEFT AARHUS, THE SUN WAS SHINING AND THE young leaves of the trees, washed clean, shifted in a gentle wind. We weren't quite as clean as everything around us, but we'd scraped the mud off our shoes and polished them, and we all wore dress-up clothes, looking forward to a meal on the ferry from Aalborg to Gothenburg in Sweden. Pete had booked us staterooms so we could get a good night's sleep which we badly needed.

Of us all, Alice was the most tired. During the rain she had been confined to the tents and bus and wanted no more to do with them. She preferred to play in the puddles. We carried her screaming and kicking into the bus, and she didn't fall asleep until ten minutes before our arrival at the ferry. Then, of course, she woke up in a bad mood. I had intended to take her to our stateroom immediately and stay with her while the others ate. But unfortunately, staterooms had not yet been assigned, so we repaired en masse to the dining saloon.

As usual, all eyes focused on us as we entered and were led to a large prominent table, where the children immediately began to fill up on bread and butter. Everybody but Alice, that is. *She* threw the bread on the floor. The waitress brought a high chair, but Alice would have none of it. Gathering her full resources, she sat on her father's lap and glared.

Jean, Mike and Ruthie didn't like anything on the menu, all two feet of it. Standard procedure. Why they pester us to take them to restaurants and why we do so, I'll never know. Since *something* had to be ordered, Pete told the patient waitress to bring meatballs and mashed potatoes all around, with shrimp cocktails first for him and me. Practically everybody objected violently.

"Quiet!" he ordered, "or I'll pitch the lot of you over the side!"

No sooner had our shrimp cocktails arrived than Alice managed one good swipe and landed her father's on the carpet. This made us *much* more interesting to the other diners. All around us I could hear chuckles and whispers of "*Amerikanere.*" At that point, a struggle between hunger and patriotism began inside me. When Alice started to cry again, patriotism won out and I made my noble offer.

"It's hopeless," I said. "I'll take her up on deck so that the rest of you can eat in peace." I waited a moment for a counter offer; none forthcoming. I reached for Alice, and she was given to me with alacrity.

"I'll come and find you as soon as I finish, and then *you* can eat," Pete called as I walked forlornly to the door, holding Alice by the hand.

Out in the corridor, she lay down and cried in front of the door to the men's room. I tried to pick her up, but she kept flattening herself to the floor with the parts of her body I didn't have hold of. Meanwhile we were impeding traffic.

"What's the matter?" the men kept asking, "Is she sick?"

"No," I kept answering, "she's just tired."

When I finally got her up on deck, I sank down on a bench and began to think about food and steaming coffee. She was limp against me, her tear-stained face covered with dirt and carpet lint. I wiped it off as gently as possible but, to my despair, she sat up and looked around. In a minute she was on her feet and dragging me to the stairs that led to the upper deck.

So we went up and down stairs a few dozen times. This was no easy matter now that we were in the middle of the Kattegat, since a strong breeze had come up and the skirt

I had on was five yards wide around the hem. I held Alice by one hand and with the other I kept trying to gather as much skirt as possible and keep it down around my knees. Thus I went up and down knock-kneed, trying to give the impression that I *loved* going up and down like that. When we reached the top for the last time, and a particularly strong breeze wrenched away my handful of skirt and flung it in my face, I gave up the pretense. Stonily, with chuckles and titters ringing in my ears, I pulled Alice to the nearest bench.

There I sat, staring out at the green rippling water, my arms full of writhing baby. Where *is* he? I kept asking myself, where *is* that man?

"Is she sick?" someone asked me for the tenth time, and I gave the stock answer, "No, she's just tired."

At last, Helen appeared, looking calm and well-fed.

"Where's your father?" I snapped. "Hasn't he finished his dinner yet?"

"Yes, but he's cleaning up Mike's and Ruthie's desserts."

After another eternity, Katy sauntered up.

"Where's your father?" I demanded.

"Oh, he's having a cigarette and another cup of coffee. He says hold the fort and he'll be right up."

Alice was limp by now, but she was still fighting sleep. Every now and then an enormous sob squeezed out. The girls had offered to take her, but I was determined to sit now until that faraway hour when my spouse should arrive. I was storing up several things to say to him. In five minutes, up he came, followed by the rest of the brood.

"Well, well," he said, "I see you have your hands full. Want me to relieve you?"

At the sound of his voice, Alice cried a heart-felt "Daddy," twisted away from me as if I were a nasty step-mother and fell into his arms. Casting a mean look in my direction, she cuddled against his chest and went to sleep.

Leaving Denmark for Sweden and Norway is like leaving a well-tended garden for places of careless variety and distant boundaries. In Denmark—"Such a *little* country!" the Danes keep telling you, half-wistfully, half-defiantly—every scrap of land is cherished; the forest preserves are neat, their dead trees reduced to squared-off piles of logs. Every open place is planted or used for grazing.

In Norway and Sweden, you can feel the land stretching away, dipping in and out of valleys, spawning forests, and even throwing away a bit here and there, since there is so much more of it.

It took a day to drive from Gothenburg to our first night's camp in Sarpsborg, Norway, near the Swedish-Norwegian border, an uneventful trip except for the two times we encountered motorcycle gangs like those sometimes seen in our own country. These youths were dressed alike in all-black uniforms with shiny helmets, and they swept by us fast, gunning their motors.

The camp in Sarpsborg was tended by an old man who was very friendly once he discovered that we were Americans and not Germans, as the D beside our license plates had first indicated.

This attitude toward Germans was very different from that of the Danes. With Germany a customer as well as a neighbor, the Danish people had relaxed to the point where they tolerated Germans in general, even *liked* individual Germans and had gone all out for the sturdy Volkswagen. They had a pet name for the plain Microbus like ours. They called it *"et halvt rugbrød,"* which means half a loaf of rye bread.

The Norwegians, on the other hand, still bitterly resented anything German and made faces at our bus on occasion. Once they ascertained we were not Teutonic, however, they softened considerably. And when we spoke Danish to them, they loved us. The old caretaker at Sarpsborg wrung Pete's hand and told him *his* Danish was much more intelligible than any Dane's.

It was still early for camping in Norway, and we were the only party established under pine trees on the hillside which sloped down to Lake Tune. There was a small dock where rowboats could be rented.

All during dinner, Helen and Katy kept their eyes on the lake and the boys rowing there, and hurried through the dishes so that they could rent a boat as soon as possible. I wasn't in favor of this at all. The lake looked deep and smoothly sinister in the still white evening. But they talked me around. They could swim, for heaven's sake! They had to grow up some time! Pete was on their side; he is all in favor of their growing up some time. So reluctantly, I agreed, and shot a sharp "Be careful!" at their backs quickly retreating down the hill.

For a while, as we put the younger children to bed and read them stories, we heard voices and the creak of oar-locks resounding from the lake. The sun went down around ten o'clock and in the twilight, alone on the hill which was made dark by the pines, we suddenly became conscious of the silence.

"Isn't it about time they were getting back?" I asked finally.

Pete and I walked down to the lake and peered up its empty stretch.

"If they'd tipped over, we'd have heard," he said un-easily. "Besides, they can swim."

We took a path that wound through trees by the shore. There was a faint sound of laughter as we came to what we had thought was the end of the lake. But another great expanse of water stretched out before us and in the middle of it, we perceived two dories, in one of which we made out the figures of Helen and Katy. In the other, there were three boys.

I was so weak with relief that my knees buckled. Then we saw what they were doing. They were circling around aimlessly, pausing every now and then to splash each other's boat to the accompaniment of a great deal of laughing and horseplay.

I jumped up and down, waving my arms and shouting to attract their attention.

"Hi, Ma and Pa!" Katy cried as she spied us. She stood up and waved while the boat rocked furiously.

"Sit down!" I screamed. "You kids come in *this minute!*"

"That's what we're trying to do," Helen called, "but the oarlock's broken." She ducked as one of the boys smacked his oar across the water, shooting a spray into her boat. "*Lad vaere!* (Lay off!)," she shrieked and aimed a spray right back at him.

"Let's go," Pete said. "We aren't doing any good here."

In camp, I put some milk on to heat for cocoa and after about fifteen minutes, Katy and Helen came back, wet but radiant.

"I thought Jens was the cutest one," Katy was saying, "but that Ole was a creep!"

From Sarpsborg, we drove to Oslo where we stayed for three days, swam in Oslo Fjord, visited the Viking Museum and Frogner Park, shopped for sweaters, looked in vain for a laundromat and washed clothes.

Then we headed west into Telemark and camped for a couple of days beside a roaring mountain stream near Rjukan. The little town of Rjukan is at the bottom of a gorge so deep that for weeks during the wintertime, no ray of sun reaches it. A funicular railway has been built up the mountain so that the inhabitants can ride up into the sunshine.

But Rjukan was of particular interest to Pete for another reason. During the war the Germans had taken over the Vermork heavy water plant located there. Heavy water is a special form of water, indispensable in studying the nuclear reactions associated with atomic energy. To extract this from ordinary water requires enormous amounts of electrical energy, and Norway, with its abundant water power, was an ideal location for such a plant.

In the middle of the war, it was completely sabotaged by the Norwegians. The Germans, however, managed to salvage one last trainload of heavy water, which they had to ferry across nearby Lake Tinnsjø which we also visited. In the middle of the lake, a time bomb went off, and now ferry, train and Germans lie at the bottom of the lake and all the heavy water has long since become diluted with ordinary light water. There was nothing of all this left to see, of course, but Pete got a good deal of pleasure from looking at where it used to be, slowly shaking his head and saying "Hmmm!"

More interesting to me was a perfect cone-shaped mountain, still white with snow, rearing above our camp. And the children were fascinated watching some farmers skin a horse.

It was Midsummer's Eve when we arrived back in Sweden. The camps overflowed with merrymakers who, weekends, come out from the towns—groups of boys in black jeans with yellow leather bindings on the pockets or in overlarge coats with flaring lapels and pants with such tight legs it seemed impossible they had managed to wiggle into them. Below the pants sprouted enormous shoes with toes so *spitz* they could have stabbed themselves. Instead of Maypoles, they brought bottles and lost no time in getting well oiled. Twice we were interested to see several boys and one girl sharing the same tent.

On the twenty-third of June, we were back in Denmark at Nivaa Camp Ground. We found the Danes getting ready to celebrate St. John's Day with bonfires and the burning of a witch. It had rained a little and the wood and the brush which had been stacked for the fire was damp. Helen and Katy went with their friends to the bonfire in Hørsholm, but the rest of us bundled up in sweaters and jackets and helped carry the wood to a forest clearing where it was heaped into a tall pyre.

At the top of the pyre was placed the witch, her face a papier-mâché mask with a long hooked nose and cruelly grinning mouth; her hair was made of black yarn and her body of old clothes stuffed with straw.

We gathered, men, women, children and babies—mostly Danes, and sat on boxes and stools in a semicircle. The three men in charge lit torches of newspaper, cautioning the crowd to move further back. We held our breath as the torches were applied, expecting a furious crackling and rush of fire all through the pile, but the scrubby wood was too damp. It caught feebly for a moment and then went out. One of the men went to get some kerosene, while the others coaxed along a small fire on one side to the accompaniment of good-natured jibes and advice from the spectators.

Then a couple of liters of kerosene were dashed on the flame and fire roared out in a blast of light and heat. It didn't last long, but the witch had caught. She was dry, and she writhed and twitched, seeming horribly alive and malevolent in the flames, her face glowing red and white with black holes for her eyes and leer. She did not die on the pyre, I gathered, but got sent back to hell, thus symbolizing the triumph of light over darkness.

The bonfire burned quickly thereafter from the top down with a fine snapping and crackling. Hymn books were passed around and we sang tender songs to Denmark while the flames became embers. By this time, the babies were asleep and the small children yawning and trying to keep their eyes open.

Tradesmen came each morning to the camp at Nivaa, selling vegetables, meats and freshly baked bread and pastries. Several families were living there for the entire summer.

One afternoon there was even a wedding reception. The bride and bridegroom were spending their honeymoon and the rest of the summer in a tent, from which the groom would commute to his job in Copenhagen. They hoped to have an apartment by fall, but meanwhile camping was cheap.

It rained off and on all that week, the wind blew, the tents swayed and creaked. The sun would come out dazzlingly for short periods and make the world seem all dramatic sky, gilding the edges of the fast-scudding clouds, pointing up their deep blue background.

While we waited for Pete's Aunt Ruth to arrive, we busied ourselves repacking our suitcases and made several trips to Copenhagen to seal up gaps in our supplies. We

also visited our favorite haunts for one last time. Sophus
Schandorph hated to see us go—he wept harder and whiter
than ever. Friends came out to say good-by. All in all, our
last week at Nivaa made us feel like the pioneers rendez-
vousing at Independence, as they readied themselves for
the trek west.

Meanwhile, I thought a lot about Ruth. She is my husband's youngest aunt, not too much older than he is, and
as he puts it, "She's a good joe!" It was going to be wonderful to have another woman along to talk to, to shop with
in the glamorous southern cities and to help me with the
work. I couldn't think of anyone I'd enjoy more than Ruth.
But she was a widow with no children and she lived alone.
Could she *really* know, I wondered, just what she was letting
herself in for?

# 10. NIGHT MUSIC

ON THE TWENTY-EIGHTH OF JUNE, PETE'S AUNT RUTH GOT
off the plane at Copenhagen's Kastrup Airport, fresh from
Edinburgh and London, looking like a younger and taller
version of the Duchess of Windsor. Her gloves and shoes
were immaculate, her hair freshly set, and her black linen
suit and white blouse hadn't been washed in cold water
and dried on a rock as our clothes obviously had. *We* all

looked as if we'd spent the last three weeks in a good stiff wind.

We stayed at Nivaa Camp Ground for another two days so that Ruth could see a little of Copenhagen. Then she buried her gloves, pumps, suit and blouse in the bottom of her one suitcase, donned pedal pushers and sandals and began to look more like the rest of us. She proved perfectly capable of taking cold showers, eating salads made in our all-purpose bucket and putting up with the children's noisy squabbling.

The day we left, Fru Svendsen invited us all to breakfast in her tiny farm home. We filled it to capacity but made no dent in her immense hospitality. Such an array of breads, pastries, cheeses, cold meats, cakes, *sodavand*, coffee and cookies, even nine of us couldn't surround. We visited the gentle Jerseys and the pampered pigs. We said good-by to Herr Svendsen and Poul. And as we left, for the first time since we were no longer employer and employee, Fru Svendsen called me *du*.

Our last night in Denmark was spent at a brand-new camp at Krusaa, a few miles from the German border. The sites were grassy and level, there was a well-stocked kiosk, clean flush toilets and even a shower room and a laundry room with hot water.

"Call this roughing it?" asked Ruth, settling down on the grass with her coffee and cigarette. "I had no idea the camps would be this good."

"Oh, just wait," I warned her. "We're going to hit some awful places before we're through. Flies, privies, broken bottles, rain, mud—"

"You make it sound so jolly," she said.

Early the next morning we left light and airy Denmark with its smooth macadam roads for the gloom-smothered landscape of Schleswig-Holstein and its bumpy cobblestones. Right away things began to be not so nice. Clouds moved in over the sun and the children began to quarrel. We'd spent our last few *kroner* on Danish pastry, and we were busy eating. All of us but Helen.

"Oh dear little Denmark," she crooned, gazing forlornly out of the back window, "will I ever see you again?"

"Oh Helen," Katy groaned, "come off it, please!"

Helen paid no attention. "If I ever see Jørgen again, he'll probably be married," she mourned. "And I'll probably be married, too!"

"Here," Katy offered briskly, with her mouth full, "have a *kringle!*"

Helen was outraged. "How can you *possibly* eat at a time like this?"

"I can eat any old time," Katy stated, "and furthermore, *I* can eat without putting on weight, which is more than some people can say!"

"Oh!" Helen exploded, "that does it. Mother! Daddy! Did you hear what she said? Now *she* can't say *she* didn't start it *this* time!"

"Oh, I did not! You criticized me first. You got mad because I offered you a *kringle*."

"Just because you have no feelings. Just because you crawl along stuffing yourself like an old caterpillar. You think *nobody* has any feelings!"

"Well, I like that! Who are *you* calling a caterpillar? You look more like a caterpillar than I do!"

In the seat behind the two girls, Mike and Jean were adding an obbligato to this duet, based on the theme of who hit whom first. I sighed and turned around. I glared, pulled in a deep breath and bellowed, "Quit!" For a small woman, my bellow is powerful. They quit! For a long time, now, I have not tried to get to the bottom of these exchanges among the children. I don't give a damn any more who starts anything.

Ruth was staring out the window, apparently fascinated with the scenery.

"This goes on a good deal of the time," I told her.

"It doesn't bother me," she said, shrugging. "I just shut it out!" She lit a cigarette.

Ruthie had crawled over the back of the seat and plopped down next to Ruth. "You sure smoke an awful lot," she piped. "This is the third one you've had since breakfast!"

"Oh, I didn't know anyone was keeping track," Ruth said mildly.

After that, the morning went smoothly enough. The sun broke through the clouds and the landscape looked a little less moody. The children urged Pete to sing his high-school song which they consider impossibly square, and he obliged. Then they played a game with roadside signs, finding words on them that contained each letter of the alphabet in turn. Ruth continued to be absorbed in the scenery and to make comments on it. It was no longer fascinating to us. By then we had rattled back and forth across northern Germany too many times to consider it thrilling.

We came to the Kiel Canal around ten-thirty and got out of the car to do it the proper honor. We sat in the high grass on its bank and watched a section of the roadway onto which cars and trucks had been driven, caged, lifted up and carried across the canal by a cable which ran under a high railroad bridge. My husband took several pictures of this operation and of the ships going through. It was a big moment for him.

We had lunch by the side of the road, opening up our folding table and stools in European fashion. Since it was Sunday, all stores except bakeries were closed, but we still had some left-over Danish cheese and ham to eat with butter and *brötchen*, the crusty German rolls. Ruth thought the bread was marvelous.

The afternoon was hot and bright. Only the streets of the towns were cool, shaded by the narrow, peaked three- and four-story buildings. People in their Sunday best strolled along window-shopping. The windows were crammed with goods; the mannequins had a solid Teutonic look about them. Ruth drank it all in eagerly.

As we drove along, we had a few frustrations. There were trains, of course. You can't drive in Germany long without being conscious of the excess of trains. Nearly every time we came to a railroad track there would be a train strung out along it, a slow train going about its business importantly, its boxcars, tank cars, refrigerator cars and gondolas crawling by like a line of turtles.

Or if there were not actually a train, we would be stopped anyhow because one was sure to be on the way. Down would come the gates just as we speeded up, thinking we'd surely beat it this time. And there would sit the man in the control booth, examining his nails or gazing at distant horizons.

While the cars and the diesel trucks piled up on either side of the track, we waited impatiently for some sign of the train—a distant whistle, a puff of smoke, anything so that we'd know we weren't going to stay there, unable to move forward or backward, until the end of time. Always, at this point, somebody had to go to the toilet.

"Well, you'll just have to wait, that's all."

"But I *can't* wait."

"Well, *what else* can you do? Do you want to run over there in those bushes?"

"Somebody might see me."

Just about the time we'd discarded all hope and *everybody* had to go, the train would appear in the distance. As it finally dragged its slow length past, we had all the time in the world to speculate on what it might be carrying. Maybe twenty boxcars filled with man-tailored suits for Frau and Fräulein in shades of shrieking green and madhouse purple. Maybe a load of caramel-colored shoes to go with the suits. Maybe twenty tons of veal cutlets. But surely a couple of dozen cars containing parts to make more trains. At last the gates would slowly lift and release us, and we would be off to look for a woodsy spot or a gas

station with toilets which nobody would need when we
found it.

We were going to spend the night in a camp near Celle.
We had been there three times before.

"You'll like Celle," I told Ruth. "It's a pretty medieval-
looking town. But the last time we were here, I ate the
greasiest sauerkraut I ever encountered!"

Since she wasn't planning to eat any sauerkraut, Ruth
admired Celle when we arrived there around four o'clock.
The camp turned out to be a bathing place for the people
of the town and they seemed to be using it, one and all.
The small scummy pond and rocky beach were thick with
bathers and sunners. Kiosk and restaurant sent out gusts of
juke-box music and stale beer; outside were piled-up banks
of boxes holding empty beer and pop bottles. The toilets
were clogged, but people used them anyway. It was too
late to look for another camp, Pete said, so we were stuck
with Celle.

However, there didn't seem to be room enough anywhere
for two tents and a Volkswagen bus. Over the heads of the
throng, a few tents poked up here and there and we charged
toward them on something that looked like a road, crossed
a ditch and plowed through to the end of the campground.

There, at the foot of a steep embankment, we found an
empty place and proceeded to set up our tents. Ruth stood
hands on hips, surveying the situation. I was awfully afraid
she was going to *like* the place or, at least, say it wasn't *too*
bad. If she did, I'd be worrying about her all the rest of the
summer, trying to figure out what she was *really* thinking.

Blankly she looked about her. The ground was littered with old cigarette packages, butts, candy wrappers and other odds and ends. Where it wasn't dusty, it was muddy; where it wasn't muddy, it was rocky. She shook her head and sighed. Her lip curled.

"Ugh!" she said, loud and clear, to my intense relief, "What a *hell* hole!" She brushed her hands together. "Well, that takes care of that," she said. "Shall we get going on the dinner?"

She peeled potatoes and sneered while I put on my *traesko* and went up to get a pail of water. There was a big mud puddle around the faucet and naturally I slipped in it and got my shoes full of mud. After Pete finished setting up the tents, the little children put on their bathing suits and he escorted them to the pond. They waded gingerly in among the flotsam, too much even for them. Some bad boys pushed them and Ruthie and Mike fell down. Mike cut his toe on a piece of glass and Ruthie gashed her knee on a rock.

Up at the kiosk Pete found they had run out of beer and Helen and Katy couldn't get any orange pop.

Dinner followed the pattern of things at Celle. The sausage that I'd bought at the kiosk was full of flour and the pastry was stale. We sat before our tents, poking at our dinner, while the tide of townspeople went out, leaving their debris behind. The last to go were two couples who had been lying on a blanket at the foot of the embankment. The girls, who were young and pretty, wriggled out of their bikinis and put on their skirts and blouses while covered by the blanket. The occupants of the tent on the other side of the field, a family of four—mother, father and two small boys, attired in identical blue and yellow fatigue suits —began to play a listless game of ball.

Hidden by bushes and trees and at right angles to the embankment we had camped against, there was a railroad track. By observing how nonchalantly campers strolled up to and disappeared into the shrubbery, we decided it was an unofficial toilet. We took a walk and discovered this was indeed the case, but you had to be careful no train was coming.

We went to bed at nine so we could get up early and leave Celle as soon as possible. I dozed, jerked awake as a train went by behind the clump of trees, and then went soundly to sleep.

I don't know what time it was when I half woke up. There was a low ominous rumbling and the ground began to vibrate slightly. At that point I came fully awake. The rumble increased in intensity, the ground shook beneath us. I broke out in a cold sweat.

Pete stirred. "What in hell?" he murmured.

"Earthquake!" I screamed above the din. "Earthquake!"

The rumbling became deafening as we ran outside, and the ground seemed to wobble beneath our feet. Ruth, Helen and Katy stumbled out of their tent. There was a blast of ear-splitting sound from the sky and we could see each other clearly in the glare. The train zoomed by on the embankment overhead, the rumble died away. We stopped trembling and started feeling foolish. I heard the children crying in the bus.

"It's all right," I called as I ran. "It was just a train!"

"I thought it was the Day of Judgment!" Ruth called.

"I thought it was the bomb!" Helen said.

"I thought it was a train," Katy said disgustedly. "*Good night!*"

# 11. A WEEK IN PARADISE

THERE ARE FEW THINGS YOU CAN'T DO WHEN YOU TAKE A camping trip in Europe accompanied by six children. You can't spend too much time inside churches, palaces and museums. The children get restless or hungry and have to go to the bathroom. For reasons I need not enumerate, you must forego all places like the Folies Bergère and that night club in Hamburg where husky ladies wrestle in mud. And, if you value your sanity and good international relations, it's best to stay out of restaurants.

I have painted the gloomy side of the picture, however. The bright side when camping in Europe with six children, is that you do not *have* to do any of these things. You can pass them up and spare your feet, your patience and your pocketbook.

From Celle, we drove south through Germany to Switzerland and down into Italy. We visited Florence, Siena, Rome and Pisa, and then followed the Mediterranean coastline into Spain.

By the time we arrived in Barcelona on July twentieth, all of us but Ruth had been camping for forty-seven days. Ruth had been with us for three weeks. We had eaten the food and drunk the water of eight different countries, swum in rivers, lakes, ponds and swimming pools, stayed up late frequently and got up early always. Nobody had been sick. Nobody had suffered so much as a stomach-ache. The only medicines we carried were aspirin and a bottle of Scotch Ruth had brought from Scotland—for adults only, to be taken on cold nights after difficult days. We hadn't used the aspirin and even the bottle of Scotch was still half full.

We were tired, however. We needed rest and relaxation before tackling the last part of our trip. Pete had provided for this by reserving rooms for a week at the Pensión Florida in Palma de Majorca. He, himself, had to fly from Barcelona to Paris for a three-day meeting of analytical chemists, but he would join us afterward in Palma.

The camp we found in Barcelona was tucked into a rather slummy section and reached by a rutted road which crossed a railroad track. A rickety gate barred it from the street. Pete did a great deal of pounding on the gate before the caretaker came to admit us. Surprisingly, the camp boasted a row of flush toilets, presided over by an old lady in black who could hardly wait for one to be vacated before she dashed in with her disinfectant and can of cleanser. The charm of the place, at first somewhat dimmed by the hardbaked, grassless dirt and the constant hum of hungry flies, was immeasurably enhanced when we discovered it possessed not only an iron and ironing board, but a small electric washing machine.

This was an opportunity not to be missed.

"I'm going to wash and iron everything in sight," I announced. "We'll all be clean and tidy for Majorca."

"Don't you want to take a look at Barcelona?" asked my husband wistfully.

After forty-seven days, most of them spent on the road, he was still eager to get into the car and go, the typical American—half-man, half-car—which has replaced the centaur. I made a remark to this effect and was accused of being half-woman, half-washing machine. Ruth, who had stayed out of this little exchange, after a discreet interval suggested the middle way. So Pete and the children departed to do the shopping and sight-seeing while Ruth and I proceeded to the washing center.

The charge for the machine was five *pesetas* to be placed in a slit in a cigar box.

We filled it up with cold water and dumped in the soap and all the clothes. Up marched the little woman in black. She stopped the machine, took out a third of the clothes and threw them into the set tub. She began to speak rapidly in Spanish.

"*No hablar español,*" I said helplessly. She wiped her hands on her apron, patted me on the back and began to speak *slowly* in Spanish with gestures.

"Well," Ruth said retreating, "while you're getting the lesson, I'll mosey along and do some ironing. *Adiós!*"

The woman started the machine again. She counted on her fingers the minutes I should let the clothes wash. Then she hurried back to her post by the toilets. At the exact time I was supposed to, I removed the clothes to the set tub, put in the others and began to scrub out a sock, rubbing it up and down on the ridged concrete side of the tub. Up came the lady in black again; she pushed me aside and seized my sock, slapped it flat on the concrete, applied a dab of soap and, holding it by the top with her left hand, began with her right to whip the toe against the rest of the sock, lightning fast, so that she worked up a stiff foam. Then she nodded at me.

"*Gracias!*" I said and reached for the sock; but she decided to do a few more before she let me try. She probably would have finished up the lot for me, but behind us rose the sound of a flushing toilet and she was off like a whippet at the sound of a gun.

While I feebly batted away at a pair of Mike's shorts, Ruth came up, a couple of freshly ironed shirts over her arm and watched me with interest.

"Getting the hang of it?" she asked.

"Frankly, no," I said. "I'm a helpless fool with a rose in my teeth. I wish I could go back to scrubbing the way I always do."

"Well go ahead and scrub," she said. "Don't look now, but Maw Perkins just went off duty."

The next morning, we left our Volkswagen and most of our suitcases in a garage and took two taxis to the airport outside of Barcelona. We were dirty only where it didn't show, there having been no shower at the camp, but we presented a clean and pressed appearance to the world at large.

The last thing my husband said to me, before we boarded the plane for Palma, was, "Don't forget to buy some paper diapers tomorrow for Alice. She's nearly out!" I nodded and juggling the baby, her bag of diapers and my handbag, mounted the steps after Ruth who had herded the others before her. I paused a moment at the top and waved wistfully at my husband, soon to be on his way to Paris.

Our party was dispersed all over the crowded plane. Ruthie and I had a seat together, and I held Alice on my lap. The engines started up, crackling like machine guns, the plane trembled like a lion having convulsions, and Alice began to scream. It didn't help a bit when the stewardess passed around pamphlets, telling in four languages what to do in case the plane ceased to function. We were flying over the sunny glitter of the Mediterranean now and, as I looked through the tiny window at the shadow of the plane far below on the water, I noticed that the landing gear had not been retracted.

The stewardess passed around glasses of powerful sherry and after a few sips, I reflected that it might, after all, be sweet to die down there in the warm blue sea among the Greek urns and the Roman coins. Alice curled up in my lap and went to sleep. Jean and Mike wandered up and down the aisle, yelling "What?" at me every time I shouted orders at them to sit down. Ruth, across the way, was being courted by a man who would later discover, when they stood up at the end of the trip, that she was a full foot taller than he was.

In no time at all we came hurtling down at Palma, shuddering, crackling and roaring. Only a person who was very sure of himself could pilot a plane in this manner. That or a mad genius. I fought hard to keep Alice inside my safety belt so that we could die together, but she wanted to stand up on the seat and look out the window at the spiky peaks rearing up to smack us.

At one o'clock, we arrived in two taxis at the Pension Florida. It was a charming villa on a hill south of the city, dripping with rosy bougainvillea and studded with hibiscus. There was a shady flagstone patio, with tables and chairs invitingly arranged for repose and refreshments. This had great appeal for us at the moment, but the manager, a little sharp dart of a man named Mr. Van der Snick, had other ideas. He wanted us to get on a bus that very afternoon and take a three-hour drive down the coast to his *other* pension which, he said, was in a tiny village and much better for the children.

"I don't understand," I said. "My husband made reservations for *here!*"

"Ah yes," said Mr. Van der Snick, "but here is not so good for children. You see? Here is no beach and only a small swimming pool, and what can they do here?"

"That isn't what your circular says," retorted Ruth. "Your circular says luxurious pool, proximity to sandy beaches, Spanish dances two evenings a week!"

He shrugged. "For the beaches you must take a long streetcar ride to one and the second you reach by motor launch. But our *other* pension is right *on* the beach! You can wear your bathing suits directly from your rooms. Believe me, ladies, you would like it very much better!"

"Is there a bullfight down there?" Katy asked.

"Bullfight?" Mr. Van der Snick was shocked. "Now what would a sweet girl like you want with a bullfight?"

"I want to *see* it—that's all."

"I don't know what to say," I sighed. "My husband is in Paris for three days and he plans to join us *here.*"

"That can be taken care of."

"But a three-hour bus ride!" I protested. "Now? When we're all dead tired and hungry. Besides—" I hesitated.

"Yes?" asked Mr. Van der Snick.

I had been going to say that we probably wouldn't be able to buy paper diapers for the baby in a small village. But it seemed a silly thing to mention just then. "Never mind," I mumbled.

"I'll give you all box lunches!" he persisted.

"No!" Helen said. "I want to go shopping in Palma."

"I want to see the bullfight," Katy insisted.

"I'm hungry," said Mike.

"Alice needs her pants changed, Ma," Jean informed me.

"Does this mean," Ruth asked, "that you *don't* have rooms reserved for us here? Is there a Better Business Bureau in Palma?"

"Ladies, ladies," the manager said wearily, "I *have* rooms for you, not here at the pension but in the annex!"

"Where's the annex?" Ruth asked sharply, "a three-hour bus ride away?"

"It's just down the street. I'll have the boy take down your bags. Now you want full pension, of course?" He drew a pad toward him and looked up expectantly.

"Well, no," Ruth said, "we'd like half pension. We want to try some of the Palma restaurants."

Mr. Van der Snick threw up his hands and had a fit. So we hastily signed up for full pension and soon were following a boy who was trundling our bags down the street in a wheelbarrow. Alice was too tired to walk, so I carried her.

It was very hot. There was scarcely a hint of green along the street, and the sun struck and glared off the hard surfaces of stone, tile and stucco. Nothing stirred but a cat, one eye bloody and dangling, who crept along in a daze, following a thin line of shade.

"Ugh!" said Ruth, gathering Mike and Ruthie close to her. "Don't look, kids." But of course that made them stare in fascination.

"This is a fine how-do-you-do," I said. "Now I know what they mean by hard-headed Dutchmen."

"Mother!" Helen flashed. "You can't proceed to indict a whole people just for the sins of one."

"Not *now*, Helen!" I said firmly. I was preparing myself for the annex. The *annex!* And we all looked so nice, and the children had been on their best behavior, too. They had stood, patiently, their beautiful eyes blinking with heat and weariness, while that man had as much as said he didn't *want* them. I held Alice tight against me and rubbed my cheek in her soft, damp hair.

We stopped at a tall apartment house rising blankly from the street. The boy opened a door into a dark, tiled hall, and then through the arched doorway opposite, we saw paradise—Spain in a travel folder or a dream. There was a courtyard of red tiles into which was set a pattern of figured tiles. In the middle of the courtyard there were three flower beds, the larger sporting a fountain, and in them bloomed pink and yellow cannas, small lime trees in fruit and flower, and pink hibiscus, all bordered with star jasmine. Bougainvillea lay glowing red on the tile roofs of the two-story apartment houses which lined the courtyard. The deep balconies of the second stories were as large as rooms and were hung with bamboo shades. We had a suite of rooms, not elegant but clean and comfortable, on the first floor of the side that faced west. There was a living room and two baths, one with a *tub*.

We washed, then walked up to the pension for lunch and afterward went willingly to bed, shades drawn against the sun, and lay as still as possible for the rest of the afternoon. There wasn't a sound to disturb us.

But at six o'clock everything came to life. The woman across from us strode out, singing in an operatic voice and was joined by another woman on a balcony. All the doors were left open, and we could peek into the kitchens that bordered the courtyard. The one opposite us was cool with blue tile and an array of gleaming copper pots. Our children, who had barely picked at their lunches, were ravenous now in the cool of the evening. Dinner at the pension was not served until eight-thirty. So we took a little walk and found a small East Indian place that served us beefsteaks.

This did not endear us to the manager of the pension the next morning when we showed up for breakfast. He was lying in wait for us outside the lobby. We had caused him to waste food, he said, and he couldn't run his pension that way. Well, we replied, we were sorry to have given him any inconvenience, but we hadn't thought it mattered. After all, we *were* paying full pension. We had tried hard not to, but we were.

He shrugged. Now, could he interest us in some tours? he asked. There was a great variety of them to suit any taste and pocketbook.

No, thanks, we said, we wanted to knock about by ourselves, swim, sun bathe, and take it easy.

He was incredulous. He didn't understand Americans who didn't want to take *tours*. He shrugged again and hurried into the lobby after telling us where to find the streetcar going to downtown Palma.

We'd been saving our money to buy things there—sandals, fans, costume jewelry and Spanish dolls. Katy and Helen had five dollars apiece, given them by Skilly and Hosmer Stone, to be spent on buying Majorca Christmas presents for themselves. I, of course, had to buy paper diapers.

The streetcar resembled the Toonerville Trolley, short and rickety. Everybody packed in goodnaturedly—there always seemed to be room for one more—and the conductor squirmed among us, collecting fares and making change. People obligingly handed coins and tickets back and forth and supported each other going around corners. Priests in round hats were absorbed in their breviaries. Ladies with glossy, elaborate hairdos wore lace church shawls and carried fans. The streetcar dawdled along for awhile, picking up more passengers and edging around corners and southbound streetcars. Then came a magnificent open stretch which we took full tilt, all of us feeling the gay abandon of the steepest drop on the roller coaster.

We disembarked dizzily at the Plaza. This is the place in Palma where old black automobiles are put out to pasture, and a beautiful old age it is for them. They are loved, tenderly shined and polished, and driven slowly around the Plaza. Thus they linger far past every expectation into the evening of life—stately Pierce Arrows, Hupmobiles, La-Salles, Packards and Maxwells—admired by the coffee sippers and ice-cream eaters sitting in the cafés lining the Plaza. There was also much else of interest there: book and magazine stands, toy sellers, ice-cream sellers, dogs, cats, pigeons, girls opening and closing fans.

"I'll go and buy those diapers before we do anything else," I said, "and get it off my mind."

"Oh, why don't you wait," Ruth asked, "and get them later? You don't want to carry those clumsy boxes around all day."

"I'll feel better if I get them now," I said virtuously. "Besides, you never know when you're going to run into the siesta."

"We'll stay here on the Plaza and wait for you," Ruth said.

Walking determinedly to a large tourist agency on the Avenida Generalissimo Franco, I had my procedure well planned.

"I don't want any information about travel or tours or anything like that," I told the man in the agency nervously. Expecting to be greeted by a woman, the man, aristocratic-looking and formal, didn't seem to me the type to know about paper diapers. Where could you rent a Rolls-Royce or charter a plane for Madrid?—That was the kind of question he was used to answering. Oh well, I thought, plunge in.

"Can you tell me where I can buy paper diapers?" I asked in a small voice.

He knit his brows. "I do not understand," he said. "What is that word again?"

"Diapers," I sighed. "Of paper. For a baby."

"Ah! Of course. Something for a baby! But I don't

know—diaper? How do you spell it?"

"D-I-A-P-E-R," I spelled, feeling more and more foolish.

"Diaper! Di-ap-er." He shook his head. "I'm sorry that I am so stupid. What is it for?"

"They are little things that you put around here on the baby," I told him, showing him delicately on myself.

"Oh! They are what you call pants?"

"Not exactly—" I sighed. "Do you have a dictionary? Or is there some lady I could talk to?"

"Of course," he assured me sympathetically. "You must excuse me. I don't know much about babies!" He disappeared into the back office.

In desperation I took my useless Spanish phrase book out of my bag. Of course it would not boast anything so practical as the Spanish word for diaper, but I riffled through it anyway, just to pass the time. I found information on how to cook a lobster. It must be alive when it is killed. I found how to ask for a good hotel and how to get my shoes shined and not too much starch in my shirts. I crammed the blasted thing back into my bag. Some day, I thought, I am going to write phrase books myself, with words in them like *diaper*.

At this point the travel agent emerged from the back room with a girl and a Spanish-English dictionary. "Will you spell that word again?" he asked. I took the book, found the word and passed it back to the girl.

"Oh!" she said, her eyes dancing. She laughed and turned to the man. "*Pañal!*"

"Aieee!" he said, clapping his hand to his forehead and

taking two steps toward the back room. "*Pañal* . . . diaper, diaper, *pañal!* I am ready for anything."

"You want a children's shop," the girl told me. "I will give you the addresses of some."

I felt stupid. Why hadn't I asked for a children's shop in the first place? Perhaps because at home I bought paper diapers in the drugstore. And in Rome and Copenhagen, I'd bought them in a department store.

The girl accompanied me now to the door of the agency, handed me the addresses and pointed me in the right direction. She gave me some complicated instructions which I couldn't follow after the first two turns.

When I arrived at the second street which I was supposed to turn into, it didn't look like a street at all. It looked more like an alley, very narrow, with no motor traffic. So I went on to the next street. That looked like an alley, too, and I turned back to the second. I had gone a few more steps when I suddenly realized that I didn't know whether I was to take the first right turn or first left turn. So I stood there holding my paper, looking helpless. (After living twelve years in Los Angeles, I still can't manage to find my way around any place but Santa Monica. Any farther afield, and my husband has to draw me a map.) At last a boy stopped to help me.

After I pointed to the first address, he gave me copious directions in Spanish with gestures. I understood only the gestures. But they helped. I went in the direction his finger pointed, stopped just around the corner and corralled a passing señora. Proceeding in this manner, I eventually found the children's shop. Of course I could get diapers there, the saleslady said; it would take a week since they must be hemmed by hand. She didn't know anything about *paper* diapers, but perhaps I could find them in a ready-made shop.

So finally, by once more following pointing fingers, I arrived at the second children's shop. They had never heard of paper diapers either, but possibly I could find them in a *farmacia*—drugstore. I had no trouble in finding a *farmacia* all on my own. In Spain, such shops still exhibit bottles of blue and red water. Unfortunately the *farmacia* was closed, but peering through the glass I discovered on a shelf, boxes of what looked like paper-diaper pads.

Eureka! I breathed a sigh of relief.

"Avenida Generalissimo Franco, *por favor?*" I asked of a passing señor. He pointed and I was off.

It was nearly lunchtime when I got back to the Plaza. In the meantime the others had done some shopping of their own. Helen had bought herself a fan, while Katy had spent her Christmas money in an antique store on a medal and an enormous crystal teardrop from a chandelier. They were all hard at work licking ice-cream cones. We considered having our lunch in a café on the Plaza, but we were too afraid of Mynheer Van der Snick's righteous wrath, so we took the trolley back to the pension.

Lunch was *arroz con pollo* in which the children managed to find chicken feathers. Helen felt a bit sick afterward, so she lay down, but the rest of us spent the afternoon at the pool. By four o'clock we were groggy with the sun and drifted back to the annex. Helen, we found, had been making frequent trips to the bathroom.

"Maybe it's the water," I said worriedly.

"Maybe it's the chicken feathers," Helen retorted. "I don't want any dinner, Ma. Do you think *he*'ll be mad?"

"I don't care if he *is* mad!" I said. "We can't arrange our whole vacation to suit Mr. Van der Snick!" I was worried. Mike looked green and listless. He sat on a chair and leafed through a Spanish comic book. "Are *you* getting sick too?" I asked.

"I don't feel good," he said. "I don't want any dinner either!"

At eight-fifteen, six of us made our silent way up to the pension. We had left Mike sound asleep and apparently a little feverish. It was really too hot to tell. We ignored the *antipasto*, played with the bean soup and hacked with no enthusiasm at the thin, tough steaks. But we all drank quantities of coke which was not included in the pension rate. Halfway through dinner, the lights flickered out. The dining terrace overlooked the whole city which was all dark now, too. The waiters lit candles stuck into the necks of bottles and in ten minutes, the lights came on again.

That night it was too hot to sleep. I was far too disturbed for sleep anyway. Helen was feeling much better, but Mike was spending most of his time in the bathroom. Oh, everybody gets the trots in this climate, I told myself, there's nothing to worry about. But it was a dismal prospect just the same. A week with nothing to do but relax in this earthly paradise and everybody gets sick! Alice was whiny and restless, what with Mike plodding in and out of the bathroom, so I took her in bed with me. She flopped from stomach to back to stomach again, giving little moans. Oh my God, I thought, not Alice, too. And I don't have any diapers yet!

In the morning she was bright-eyed and full of energy, but Katy was sick and Helen still didn't feel like eating, either. Just five of us went up to breakfast. I told the manager that three of our party were sick and I couldn't be sure how many of us would be taking meals from now on. He was resigned, even sympathetic. If we needed a doctor, he said, just let him know.

I asked him for a drugstore nearby and he told me of one. So, while Ruth took the children back to our rooms for their bathing suits, I walked down a long flight of stairs and around the corner to the drugstore. If they had boxes that looked like paper diapers in one drugstore, they had them in all, I reasoned, and I'd sure feel a lot better about facing the future with a good nearby source of supply.

"*Pañales de papel, por favor,*" I told the druggist confidently. He wrinkled his brow. My heart sank. He shrugged and made me understand that I could get *pañales* only in a children's shop. I thanked him as my eyes roamed the entire *farmacia*, searching for a pile of boxes that might contain paper diapers. He willingly showed me everything I was looking at. He had a rather surprising stock, all sorts of things I thought you'd find only in an American drugstore and fully as many patent medicines with illustrated directions explicit enough for me to understand, even in

Spanish. But he was awfully sorry that he didn't have paper diapers; he saw how this lack distressed me.

The only thing to do now was to ride into Palma. Helen said she was well enough to go with me and, besides, she wanted to look for a bathing suit. Ruthie, Jean and Alice were still frisky and having fun in the pool. Ruth was taking a sun bath while she minded them.

All during our ride I worried that I wouldn't be able to find that certain drugstore again. But, miraculously, I found it right away in all that winding maze of streets and little shops. Unfortunately, however, it was still closed. Through the glass I peered, seeking again the pile of boxes against the wall that *might* contain paper diapers. I have good eyes, and managed to read the label. *Pañuelos de papel*, it said.

I leaned against Helen in excited relief. "That's it," I cried. "Read it, honey. It does say *pañuelos*, doesn't it?"

"But *pañuelos* isn't *pañales*," she objected.

"Never mind," I said, "it's near enough. Lots of words in English can be spelled two different ways. And remember, Helen, the word for *paper* diapers *could* be just a bit different from the word for *cloth* diapers!"

She eyed me skeptically. "And you *could* be fooling yourself too, Ma," she said.

I sighed. "Helen," I said sternly, "from now on keep still. Whatever it is, I'll take it."

She shrugged. We plodded on in silence looking for a drugstore that was open. To be sure, I also had my doubts about the meaning of *pañuelos*. But the pressing need for them had blotted everything else from my mind.

"What else could they be?" I demanded indignantly as we came to a window flaunting blue and red flasks.

"I didn't say a word, Ma." Helen protested meekly.

"*Pañuelos de papel?*" I asked the man behind the counter. He didn't bat an eyelash.

"*Para damas o para hombres?*" he inquired. This stopped me cold. I couldn't begin to fathom what might be the difference between diapers for men or for women. *For women or men?* He went to a shelf and brought back two boxes of different sizes of the now familiar type.

"*Para damas,*" he said, pointing to the smaller, "*y para hombres,*" pointing to the larger. He smiled, awaiting my decision.

"Well, I don't know," I said in confusion, turning to Helen, "if Alice is going to have diarrhea, I guess I should get the larger—"

Helen snorted. "Hadn't you better find out what they *are* first?"

"I'm not going all through *that* again!" I snapped. "For better or worse, I'm going to take them, whatever they are, hope for the best and get out. I'm sick and tired of being a crazy American!"

"*Para hombres!*" I said firmly. "*Cinco, por favor!*"

"*Cinco?*" he asked, looking startled.

"You're going to buy *five*, and you don't even know what you're getting?" screeched Helen. "Oh, Mother!"

We went to a café on the Plaza and had an orangeade, the package of whatever it was still unopened. I hadn't the courage to find out.

"Well, if *you* aren't going to open them, *I will!*" Helen said. "They can't be anything so awful."

"They just might be!" I quivered, thinking of all kinds of things that shouldn't be opened in public—trusses, for instance, or—no! This was Spain, after all, and besides they were something made of paper! Clinging to that last thought, I watched hypnotized, as Helen tore open a package and drew forth what appeared to be a paper napkin.

We laughed until the tears came.

"Oh, these Spanish!" I sighed at last. "Why would they have two different sizes of napkins for men and women?"

"They aren't napkins, Ma, they're *handkerchiefs*," Helen informed me. "See? They've got what looks like fancy hemming around the edge."

I examined one. It was very soft and thick, at least four ply. I took three of them, shook them out, put them together and folded in the opposite corners. This made a very acceptable diaper pad. I waved it in front of Helen's nose.

"Well, I have to hand it to you, Ma," she said. "Pick up the marbles!"


We didn't get back to the pension with the handkerchief diapers any too soon. Alice had already begun to have diarrhea. Jean wasn't feeling well either. Alice was feverish by evening, so we had the doctor for her. Nothing to worry about, he said, just acute enteritis.

"Does she take medicine well?" he asked.

Alice had never taken anything before except cough syrup and half an aspirin crushed up and covered with honey. Nevertheless, she opened her mouth for the doctor and swallowed a tablespoon of some thick white substance which she promptly gave right up all over the bed.

We were in for it! Four of us were sick and by midnight I realized that I was next on the list. The Spanish plumbing got a terrible workout and gave up. Fortunately, all the people in the court had proved to be most sympathetic and helpful. There was one man there who shared a language with me. We spoke in French and he assured me that his family would be available any time we needed them and that I should not hesitate to wake him even in the middle of the night. If we wanted anything from a *farmacia*, a boy with a bicycle would go for us. According to local custom, only one *farmacia*, a different one each night, was open after six.

For two days we were kept busy in various ways. I always had the bathtub full of soaking clothes and clothes were drying on hangers all over our rooms. Alice quickly ran through the five boxes of paper handkerchiefs and started on a fresh batch. She was only allowed to eat chicken soup with rice. This we managed to buy from the nearby East Indian restaurant. She refused to take her medicine, so we attempted to hide it under the rice. Her eyes pierced the rice every time, and she would dart sometimes piteous, sometimes furious looks at us for trying to fool her. At last we gave up and she ate the soup happily.

In the stifling evenings, Ruth and I consoled ourselves

with sherry and wondered wistfully what Pete was doing in Paris. I could hardly wait for his return so that I could get some rest. By Thursday, however, everyone was well. Pete was due that afternoon and we planned big things. We'd go to the beach the next day. Maybe we'd take a bus to Formentor. Or we'd go to see some Spanish dances. The dancers advertised by the Pension Florida, had long ago terminated their engagement.

"Anything," I said to Ruth, "so long as we get out of this smelly place!" There were tears of joy and relief in my eyes when Pete arrived. He looked big, solid and dependable, and we all hung on him.

"Take it easy, kids," he said. "I don't feel so good! I think I'm going to be sick!"

I stared at him, outraged. "Don't you dare!"

Fortunately, he was acutely sick for only a day. On Saturday, Helen and Katy went shopping in Palma, while the rest of us took a motor launch to a beach with white sand and water so clear, warm and silky that it was worth waiting for. That evening at the pension, all was back to normal. Nine of us went up to dinner and the lights flickered out on schedule. And after the candlelight period, I discovered in my *paella* a tiny piece of tentacle with minute round suckers on its netherside and almost got sick all over again.

On Monday, our stay in the Mediterranean paradise ended as it began, with Mynheer Van der Snick having a fit because Pete insisted on paying our bill in *pesetas* which we had bought cheaply in Geneva instead of in dollars.

At five that evening, we were again outside the camp in Barcelona, beating on the gate. The first person we saw when we had passed the barrier was the little old guardian of the toilets. A look of amazement passed over her face as she caught sight of us. "*Ai de Dios!*" She cried in dismay and threw her apron over her face. But when she cast it down again, she was laughing.

# 12. FOOD FOR THOUGHT

THE NEXT NIGHT FOUND US CAMPING IN A PEACH ORCHARD near Lérida, Spain. We were told by its owner that it was going to be a magnificent camp next year but that he hadn't got around to building it yet. With pride, he showed us the cement sinks which would be complete with taps and water next summer. Meanwhile, we'd have to tramp up the road half a mile to his gas station to draw water and to wash. He had a huge swimming pool there too, which his campers could use.

After we had cleared our site of enough rocks and debris to set up our tents, we put on our bathing suits and went up to the gas station for a cooling dip. The pool was there all right and large enough for the Olympics, but it was still in the process of being filled. The method the Spaniard was using to fill it, a slow trickle from a leaky hose, convinced us that his pool would be full by the time his camp was completed—namely, next year. Disgruntled we trudged back to the orchard and ate his peaches in the shade.

In 1957, camping was new in Spain and there were no camps near Madrid or below. So, after a stop at Zaragossa, we cut back to France through Navarre and spent our last night in Spain near San Sebastian.

In the French camps along the Bay of Biscay, we were afforded intimate glimpses of French family life. The broad housewives sat in their slips enjoying the cool of the evening or made their toilettes at the open-air sinks, paying absorbed attention to every inch that showed, particularly their armpits. It was easy to find a vacant shower in a French camp, but you had to fight your way to the sinks.

By this time, early August, I'm afraid Ruth and I no longer bothered much about cooking dinner. Cold meats, a salad, bread, cheese and fruit often sufficed. One evening in Bergerac, we set up next to a large French family. They all slept together in a truck, but they had provided them-

selves with a complete kitchen and dining room under a
huge awning. We made a quick supper from a couple of
cans of *cassoulet* and a salad, but our neighbors had evidently been cooking all afternoon. Long after we had
washed our dishes and were sitting idly before our tent,
Madame was still chopping up vegetables and throwing
them into the pot. She was a slow-moving woman with a
fine mustache, and on each portentous trip from chopping
board to kettle, she threw a sneer in our direction. We
couldn't blame her. The aroma from her camp was in-
describable. Her family sat down to eat around eight o'clock
and when we retired two hours later, they were still at it.

This episode must have aroused the gourmet in me, for
the next morning in Perigueux, I was seized with a longing
to buy a large can of genuine *foie gras* with truffles. Even
in truffle country, this was expensive and our money was
running out, so I felt compelled to stand in the store, flanked
by my husband and two oldest daughters, and dither for
awhile. Ruth and the younger children waited impatiently
in the bus.

"It does seem rather selfish of me," I remarked, turning
the can over and over and reading the label several times
to be sure it contained unadulterated goose liver. "I really
shouldn't spend five dollars on this when I'm the only one
that wants it. Five dollars will buy us food for a whole
day."

"Well, make up your mind one way or the other," said
Pete. "Probably tastes just like liverwurst, anyway."

"On the other hand," I said firmly, "it wouldn't be selfish if I saved it until we got home and then served it at a cocktail party!"

"Well then, buy it!" Pete said. "Only let's do something besides stand here all morning!" This was the wrong thing for him to say.

"I *won't* buy it!" I announced, laying it down. "I only wanted it for sentimental reasons, anyway. I can remember so clearly my grandmother telling me when I was a little girl how they used to force-feed the geese in Lorraine—"

"Mother," pleaded Helen, displaying the correct feeling in her voice, "please buy it. It isn't selfish. You *deserve* it!" She cast an indignant glance at her father and ostentatiously began to fumble in the enormous complicated leather bag she'd bought in Florence. The bag had everything in it but money. We all knew she'd spent her last franc on a carved *sabot*.

"Oh Helen," said Katy, "come off it, please!" But Helen's gesture had had the desired effect on her father.

He sighed. "Sooner or later you're going to buy a can of goose liver, so let's get it over with now!" He retrieved the can, plunked it down on the counter before the patient salesgirl and hurriedly counted out the money.

"Happy?" he asked as we walked back to the bus.

I shrugged my shoulders. The decision had been his, not mine, and I could enjoy the *foie gras* with a clear conscience. Some day I am going to sit down quietly and figure out why I am compelled to set up these little dramas— whether it's a martyr complex, a reaction against the male for being the provider, or sheer niggardliness. On the other hand, if I ever begin to understand myself, there is the danger that my husband will also understand me. Then he might not put up with it.

Meanwhile I had the *foie gras*. I set the can in the open dashboard compartment and every now and then as we chugged along, I released my eyes from the rugged green, the crusty old rocks and roofs of the middle of France and let them rest on it lovingly. I didn't intend to eat it in the foreseeable future. I would save it for a very special occasion, just what, I couldn't imagine. When we got home, I would place it on the top shelf of the can cupboard, along with the green turtle soup and the Beluga caviar which were too good to eat, because if you ate them, you didn't have them anymore.

I thought of the can cupboard, and then I thought of our nice big kitchen at home with the mixer, the blender, the refrigerator, the electric washer and the dryer. I thought of the bathtub and a lavish flow of hot water. I thought of the patio and the back yard and the three raccoons that came up from the canyon every night to be fed.

We were all thinking of home. French red squirrels in the pines reminded us of gray squirrels in the eucalyptus trees. The mountains of the Massif Central made us think of our own mountains which, of course, are higher. When we crowded in with the French to see the cave paintings at Lescaux, I was conscious of a feeling of relief that back home *our* people didn't depend so much on garlic.

Our last night in France we spent at Vienne on the

Rhone River. There we saw the Roman temples, but primarily we remember the camp at Vienne as the one place in France where no wine was available, only beer.

The next three days we camped at Geneva and it was there we said goodby to Ruth. Wistfully, I sat in the tent and watched her retrieve her suit, girdle and nylons from the bottom of her bag. The suit was rather creased from its long repose. She shook and smoothed it out.

"Oh, well, she said, "I'll have it pressed in the hotel tonight."

Already she belonged to a world of clean beds, hot baths and dinners nicely served. After a night in a hotel, she was bound for a week in Paris and Amsterdam.

We deposited her at the Hotel Angleterre, and she stood and waved at us until we rounded the corner. Right away, the bus didn't feel comfortable without her.

"What do you think Ruth's doing now?" Jean asked glumly after a long silence.

"I'll bet she's sitting in a nice soft chair, having a beer," Katy said, "and thinking about what to order for dinner. What are *we* going to have for dinner, Ma?"

"Noodle soup and cold cuts," I snapped.

"Not *again!*" groaned Mike.

"Well, if you don't like it, you can just eat bread and cheese," I replied.

"Gee, wouldn't it be nice if Ma broke out her goose liver tonight?" Katy asked. "How about it, Ma?"

I cast a long reproachful glance back at her. I felt lonesome and drained of all strength.

"You're just trying to make her feel guilty again," Helen said, "and I don't think you should at a time like this, with Ruth staying at a hotel and all."

"I wish we could ever stay in a hotel," Jean threw in. "I wish we could ever sleep in something besides this old bus."

"You can all sleep in the tents tonight," Pete stated, but this offer elicited no cheers.

Pete tried again. "Do you know what we'll be doing tomorrow?"

Nobody cared to ask.

"Tomorrow, we'll be riding along beside the Alps. We'll be able to see the Jungfrau!"

"Who cares about those old Alps?" Mike jeered, and the rest of them began to giggle.

I turned on Pete, too. "I wish you wouldn't always look so determinedly on the bright side," I said. "It gets rather nauseating."

He scratched his head, sighed and stared blankly through the windshield. Then he got mad.

"Well, nauseating or not, somebody has to do it," he shouted. "We've got about eight more days before we get on the ship at Bremerhaven. Eight days—that's all! And after that, we'll never have to spend another night in a tent for the rest of our lives. You'll get motels and restaurants until they're coming out of your ears on the way home. And I know what it'll be like! 'Oh Daddy, do we have to eat in another old restaurant?' 'Oh Daddy, I don't like the pickles in the tunafish sandwich.'"

"All right, all right," I said hastily, "slow down or you'll miss the road to the camp!"

He made a giant turn. "Keep still, now, all of you. Because I'm going to enjoy this week, by God, and I don't give a damn whether the rest of you do or not!"

Chastened, we enjoyed the ride up to Berne the next day with the sun sparkling on the snowy Alps, and we fervently admired the Jungfrau. I craned back after it for miles. At Berne, we had a beautiful grassy camp with showers. Everybody was being nice.

The following day was sultry, not the sort of day to spend our last Swiss money on chocolate, but we did exactly that. By the time we reached the German border, children and bus were plastered with it. Dark clouds began to gather while we waited at customs, and nervously we watched the car ahead of us get searched and relieved of a good many interesting bottles and other items. I began to worry that we'd bought more than our limit of chocolate, but after one look into the bus, the customs officer waved us on. He probably figured we had troubles enough.

At Schopfheim, twenty miles into the Black Forest, the dark clouds finally clashed together and hurled fat drops against the windshield. The drops soon became slashing sheets which slid down the windows. In the hot closeness of the bus, the children began to squirm and complain.

"Why does it *always* have to rain?" Ruthie complained.

"It doesn't always have to rain," explained Pete. "It just seems that way. This is coming down too fast to last long. It'll probably clear up before we get to the campground."

"Daddy," pleaded Helen, "do we *have* to camp tonight? Can't we stay in a hotel? *Please?*"

I glanced hopefully at his face. It seemed to me to be softening. I saw his lips move in calculation, and then his jaw tightened.

"Can't we, Daddy? Can't we stay in a hotel?"

"No, we *can't* stay in a hotel!" he thundered. "Why are you so afraid of a little rain? We said we were going to camp this summer, and, by God, we're going to camp!" His jaw was set sternly. There was silence for awhile except for the hissing of the wheels and the roaring of the torrents.

"A *little* rain, he says!" Helen dropped into the silence. There were mutterings and giggles.

"Daddy's a cheapskate," Mike ventured softly. The giggles increased. "Daddy's a pinchpenny," Ruthie offered more boldly. A smile appeared on Pete's face.

"Really, honey," I said, "I don't see why we can't break down just this once and find a hotel. We're all so tired and hot—"

"Do you want to know how much money we've got this side of the ocean?" he demanded.

"No!" I yelled. "Don't tell me. I don't want to hear."

"Well, then," he said.

I buried my face in Alice's hair. It was sweaty and smelled of chocolate, and I wiped a few tears on it.

"I never should have done it," I said loudly. "I *knew* I shouldn't have done it!"

"Done what?" asked Pete.

"Bought that goose liver!" I murmured in a trembling voice.

"What?" he asked outraged. "Did you say goose liver?"

"Well, it wasn't only the goose liver," I managed hastily. "There was that skirt in Spain and all that stuff in Florence!"

He groaned.

"There goes Ma's goose liver again!" Katy remarked. "Regular as clockwork!"

"You keep still with your sarcasm," I shouted. "Nobody in this family has any respect."

"I'm getting hungry," Mike announced.

"Hungry!" I exclaimed. "How can you be hungry? You kids have eaten four pounds of chocolate in the last two hours."

"Not quite," said Pete wearily. "They've smeared most of it on the bus. How in hell did it get on the steering wheel? Somebody hand me a Kleenex."

At last we emerged from the forest onto a road full of ruts and rushing water which sloped down into what was once a grassy meadow. We had arrived at Titisee campground, described in the German camping club booklet as being complete with kiosk, potable water and toilets which did not flush. A number of bedraggled tents appeared to float on the campground which was surrounded by a ditch filled to the brim with water just beginning to slop over. The roadbed crossing it had been strengthened by planks which now bobbled like corks.

On the other side of the ditch, veered off from the road, was an Opel up to its hubcaps in mud. Two men were packing straw beneath its wheels. They looked up as we approached.

"Hold on!" yelled Pete, not slackening speed a bit.

"No, Pete, no!" I shouted, grabbing Alice tightly and bracing my feet. "Don't do it!"

But he launched the bus onto the planks and across the ditch by sheer nerve and momentum—there certainly was nothing else to drive on. The two men with the Opel cheered and waved their arms as we spurted past them to higher ground and stopped.

"Well," said Pete, "here we are!"

Nobody else said anything. We surveyed the depressing scene. All tent flaps were tightly zipped. The small kiosk was boarded up. A couple attired in raincoats and rubber boots sloshed through the mud with a pail of water between them. Back by the ditch, one of the men got into the Opel and vainly whirred the motor. One plank and then another left the roadbed and floated slowly down the ditch.

"Here we are!" repeated Pete. "When the rain lets up a bit, we can find some high ground and pitch a tent." There was silence. It was beginning to get chilly in the car with the motor off.

"There was this girl in my class back home," Helen said plaintively, "Vikki something, and her father was a producer. When *they* went to Europe, they stayed in hotels!"

"Well, we stayed in hotels," I offered, "last fall and in Majorca."

"They stayed in *good* hotels! Like in Paris, they stayed

at the George V!"

"Bully for them!" Pete said.

"I wish we could have been in a hotel tonight," Ruthie said in a tiny voice.

"Even if we can't stay in a hotel, can't we at least *eat* in a restaurant?" Mike asked.

"Do you see any restaurants around here?" Pete inquired. We all looked around again. The last plank had left the roadbed for parts unknown and roadbed and ditch had merged into a little pond. It was obvious that there would be no more driving to and from the campground that night. We were marooned.

"I'll tell you what we'll do," said Pete. "I'll get some water and Ma can cook us up some of that Swiss noodle soup."

*"Here? In the bus?"* I cried.

"Where else? You kids scramble back there on the deck and hand me the stove. We can set it up down there by Ma's feet."

Everyone was intrigued by this idea. It was a bit nerve-racking for me, though, keeping my feet and the baby out of the soup. We also had a box of crackers, bread and cheese, four bananas, three oranges and the remaining chocolate. After eating, we put the soup dishes outside to wash off in the rain and Pete and I drank our coffee.

Around seven o'clock, the rain petered out, and people began to emerge from their tents. The kiosk was unboarded and lighted up and we could see clearly the path to the washrooms and toilets. Some Dutch campers pointed out a comparatively high spot on which we managed to pitch one tent and the awning.

Later that evening, with the four little ones asleep in the bus, the rest of us sat at our table under the awning, waiting for the water for a pot of tea to boil.

"I'm still hungry," Helen said. "Isn't there *anything* left to eat?"

"Well, there's Ma's goose liver," Katy said. "Don't you think this is a good place to eat it, folks? Let's have a party."

I sighed. I slapped my hand down on the table. "Katy—" I began.

"Yes, Mother?" she said brightly, batting her eyelashes and all respectful attention.

"Get the *foie gras!*"

"You don't *mean* it!" she cried, jumping up. "Mother, are you sure you feel well?"

"Get it!" I pointed toward the bus.

We smeared the goose liver on soggy crackers and divided with precision the two truffles we found buried in it. I let them taste theirs first and watched their faces as they chewed. They certainly weren't ecstatic. Gingerly, I sampled mine.

"Well, who's going to say it?" I asked.

"Tastes just like liverwurst to me!" Pete said.

"You have very insensitive taste buds," I told him. "It cost five dollars!"

"But *good* liverwurst!" he said, nodding. "In fact, the *very best* liverwurst!"

Five days later, our gear packed tightly for the last time, we were in Bremerhaven, ready to board the ship. By pre-arrangement, we met Skilly and Hosmer Stone, who were also on their way home, at their hotel. We were their guests for dinner.

There we all sat at last—in a private dining room, plates of steak with fried eggs and delicious strange-looking mushrooms before us. Pete and I were eating ravenously and attempting to talk with Skilly and Hosmer and the kids were wiggling, sighing and poking suspiciously at their food.

"What's the matter with you kids anyway?" Pete asked. "You've been yelping about eating in restaurants for weeks. Eat!"

Mike made a face. "I don't like those yellow things!" he said.

"Daddy," Ruthie pleaded, "can't we *just* have some bread and cheese?"